LATIN AMERICAN POLITICAL, ECONOMIC, AND SECURITY ISSUES

CUBA IN CONTEXT

A CONSIDERATION OF ISSUES AND U.S. RELATIONS AND RESTRICTIONS

LATIN AMERICAN POLITICAL, ECONOMIC, AND SECURITY ISSUES

Additional books in this series can be found on Nova's website
under the Series tab.

Additional e-books in this series can be found on Nova's website
under the e-book tab.

LATIN AMERICAN POLITICAL, ECONOMIC, AND SECURITY ISSUES

CUBA IN CONTEXT

A CONSIDERATION OF ISSUES AND U.S. RELATIONS AND RESTRICTIONS

JANET G. CAMPBELL
EDITOR

nova publishers
New York

Library of Congress Cataloging-in-Publication Data

ISBN: 978-1-63482-985-4

Published by Nova Science Publishers, Inc. † New York

CONTENTS

PREFACE

Political and economic developments in Cuba and U.S. policy toward the island nation, located just 90 miles from the United States, have been significant congressional concerns for many years. Especially since the end of the Cold War, Congress has played an active role in shaping U.S. policy toward Cuba, first with the enactment of the Cuban Democracy Act of 1992 and then with the Cuban Liberty and Democratic Solidarity Act of 1996. Both of these measures strengthened U.S. economic sanctions on Cuba that had first been imposed in the early 1960s, but the measures also provided roadmaps for a normalization of relations dependent upon significant political and economic changes in Cuba. A decade ago, Congress partially modified its sanctions-based policy toward Cuba when it enacted the Trade Sanctions Reform and Export Enhancement Act of 2000 allowing for U.S. agricultural exports to Cuba that led to the United States becoming a major source for Cuba's food imports. This book discusses Cuba's political and economic environment; U.S. policies toward Cuba; and selected issues in U.S.-Cuban relations. This book also provides information on legislative provisions restricting relations with Cuba. It lists the various provisions of law comprising economic sanctions on Cuba, including key laws that are the statutory basis of the embargo, and provides information on the authority to lift or waive these restrictions.

In: Cuba in Context
Editor: Janet G. Campbell

ISBN: 978-1-63482-985-4

Chapter 1

CUBA: ISSUES FOR THE 114TH CONGRESS*

Mark P. Sullivan

SUMMARY

Cuba remains a one-party communist state with a poor record on human rights. The country's political succession in 2006 from the long-ruling Fidel Castro to his brother Raúl was characterized by a remarkable degree of stability. In 2013, Raúl began his second and final five-year term, which is scheduled to end in February 2018, when he would be 86 years old. Castro has implemented a number of market-oriented economic policy changes over the past several years, including an expansion of self-employment. A 2011 party congress laid out numerous economic goals that, if implemented, could significantly alter Cuba's state-dominated economic model. Few observers, however, expect the government to ease its tight control over the political system. While the government has released most long-term political prisoners, short-term detentions and harassment have increased significantly over the past several years, reflecting a change of tactics in repressing dissent.

* This is an edited, reformatted and augmented version of a Congressional Research Service publication, No. R43926, dated February 27, 2015.

U.S. Policy

Congress has played an active role in shaping policy toward Cuba, including the enactment of legislation strengthening and at times easing various U.S. economic sanctions. U.S. policy over the years has consisted largely of isolating Cuba through economic sanctions, while a second policy component has consisted of support measures for the Cuban people, including U.S. government-sponsored broadcasting (Radio and TV Martí) and support for human rights and democracy projects. For most of the Obama Administration's first six years, it continued this similar dual-track approach of isolating Cuba but reaching out the Cuban people. The Administration continued to call for the release of U.S. government subcontractor Alan Gross, imprisoned in Cuba in 2009, whose detention was an impediment to more constructive relations.

Just after the adjournment of the 113th Congress in December 2014, President Obama announced major developments in U.S.-Cuban relations that included Cuba's release of Alan Gross on humanitarian grounds and, separately, the release of a U.S. intelligence asset in Cuba exchanged for three Cuban intelligence agents imprisoned in the United States.

With these releases, President Obama then announced a major shift in U.S. policy toward Cuba, moving away from a sanctions-based policy toward one of engagement and a normalization of relations. This policy change included efforts to restore diplomatic relations; a review of Cuba's designation by the Department of State as a state sponsor of international terrorism; and an increase in travel, commerce, and the flow of information to Cuba. In order to implement this third step, the Treasury and Commerce Departments eased the embargo regulations in such areas as travel, remittances, trade, telecommunications, and financial services. The overall embargo, however, remains in place, and can only be lifted with congressional action or if certain conditions in Cuba are met, including that a democratically elected government is in place. The President maintained that the United States would continue to raise concerns about democracy and human rights in Cuba, but emphasized that the United States could do more through engagement than isolation.

Legislative Activity

The Obama Administration's shift in Cuba policy has spurred strong interest in Congress. Some Members lauded the initiative as in the best interest of the United States and a better way to support change in Cuba, while others criticized the President for not obtaining more concessions from Cuba to advance human rights. Already in the 114th Congress, several hearings have been held on the policy change, and 11 legislative initiatives have been introduced. Several bills would lift or ease sanctions: H.R. 274, H.R. 403, and H.R. 738 (overall embargo and other economic restrictions); H.R. 634; H.R. 664, and S. 299 (travel restrictions); H.R. 635 (agricultural and medical exports and travel); and S. 491 (certain embargo restrictions). Among other measures, H.R. 570 would cease Radio and TV Martí broadcasting; H.R. 654 would prohibit changes of the lease with Cuba for the Guantanamo Naval Station unless Congress authorizes such action; H.R. 738 would allow Cuban nationals to play professional baseball in the United States; and S.Res. 26 would commend Pope Francis for his role in securing the release of Alan Gross and for working to improve U.S.-Cuban relations.

INTRODUCTION

Political and economic developments in Cuba and U.S. policy toward the island nation, located just 90 miles from the United States, have been significant congressional concerns for many years. Especially since the end of the Cold War, Congress has played an active role in shaping U.S. policy toward Cuba, first with the enactment of the Cuban Democracy Act of 1992 (P.L. 102-484, Title XVII) and then with the Cuban Liberty and Democratic Solidarity Act of 1996 (P.L. 104-114). Both of these measures strengthened U.S. economic sanctions on Cuba that had first been imposed in the early 1960s, but the measures also provided roadmaps for a normalization of relations dependent upon significant political and economic changes in Cuba. A decade ago, Congress partially modified its sanctions-based policy toward Cuba when it enacted the Trade Sanctions Reform and Export Enhancement Act of 2000 (P.L. 106-387, Title IX) allowing for U.S. agricultural exports to Cuba that led to the United States becoming a major source for Cuba's food imports.

Over the past decade, much of the debate in Congress over U.S. policy has focused on U.S. sanctions, especially over U.S. restrictions on travel to Cuba. The George W. Bush Administration initially liberalized U.S. family travel to Cuba in 2003, but subsequently tightened restrictions on family and other categories of travel in 2004 because of Cuba's crackdown on political dissidents. In 2009, Congress took legislative action in an appropriations measure (P.L. 111-8) to ease restrictions on family travel and travel for the marketing of agricultural exports, marking the first congressional action easing Cuba sanctions in almost a decade. The Obama Administration took further action in April 2009 by lifting all restrictions on family travel and on cash remittances by family members to their relatives in Cuba and restarting semi-annual migration talks that had been curtailed in 2004. In January 2011, the Administration announced the further easing of restrictions on educational and religious travel to Cuba and on non-family remittances, and it also expanded eligible airports in the United States authorized to serve licensed charter flights to and from Cuba. In December 2014, just after the adjournment of the 113th Congress, President Obama announced a major shift in U.S. policy toward Cuba, moving away from a sanctions-based policy aimed at isolating Cuba to a policy of engagement and a normalization of relations. As announced, part of the President's initiative is to increase travel, commerce, and the flow of information to Cuba.

This report is divided into three major sections analyzing Cuba's political and economic environment, U.S. policy toward Cuba, and selected issues in U.S.-Cuban relations. While legislative initiatives are noted throughout the report where appropriate, a final section of the report provides a listing of bills and resolutions introduced in the 114th Congress.

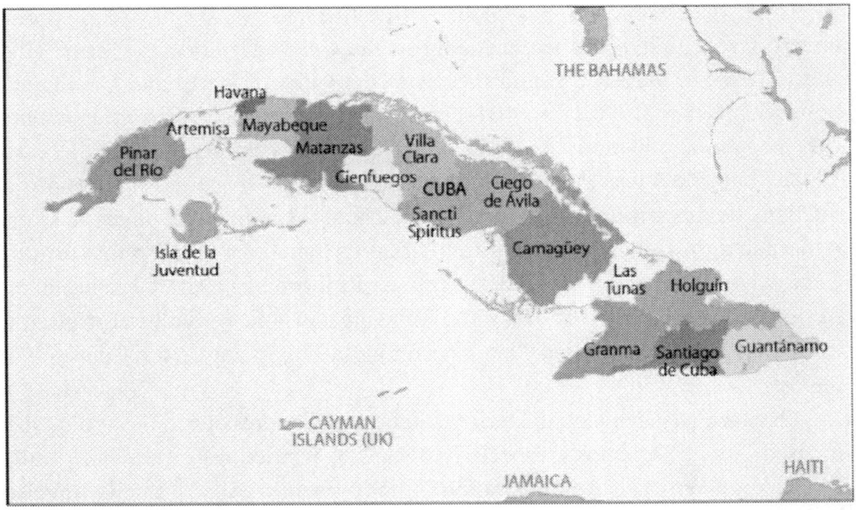

Source: CRS.

Notes: This map shows 15 provinces and the special municipality of Isla de la Juventud. See a current interactive provincial map of Cuba, showing municipalities and other information, from *Juventud Rebelde* (Cuba), available at http://www.juventudrebelde.cu/multimedia/graficos/nueva-division-politico-administrativa/.

Figure 1. Provincial Map of Cuba.

CUBA'S POLITICAL AND ECONOMIC ENVIRONMENT

Brief Historical Background[1]

Cuba became an independent nation in 1902. From its discovery by Columbus in 1492 until the Spanish-American War in 1898, Cuba was a Spanish colony. In the 19th century, the country became a major sugar producer, with slaves from Africa arriving in increasing numbers to work the sugar plantations. The drive for independence from Spain grew stronger in the second half of the 19th century, but it only came about after the United States entered the conflict when the USS *Maine* sank in Havana Harbor after an explosion of undetermined origin. In the aftermath of the Spanish-American War, the United States ruled Cuba for four years until Cuba was granted its independence in 1902. Nevertheless, the United States still retained the right to intervene in Cuba to preserve Cuban independence and maintain stability in accordance with the Platt Amendment[2] that became part of the Cuban Constitution of 1901. The United States subsequently intervened militarily three times between 1906 and 1921 to restore order, but in 1934, the Platt Amendment was repealed.

Cuba at a Glance

Population: 11.2 million (2013).

Area: 109,884 sq. km, slightly smaller than Pennsylvania

GDP: $68.23 billion (2011, current U.S. $).

Per Capita Income: $5,890 (2011, current U.S. $)

Key Trading Partners: Exports (2013): Venezuela, 43%; Canada, 8.8%; the Netherlands, 8.7%; China, 6.5%.

Imports (2013): Venezuela, 33%; China, 10.4%, Spain, 8.3%; Brazil, 4.2%; Mexico, 3.5%.

Life Expectancy: 79 years (2012)

Literacy (adult): 99.8% (2012)

Legislature: National Assembly of Peoples Power, 612 members

Sources: *World Bank; National Office of Statistics and Information (ONEI), Republic of Cuba*

Cuba's political system as an independent nation was often dominated by authoritarian figures. Gerardo Machado (1925-1933), who served two terms as president, became increasingly dictatorial until he was ousted by the military.

A short-lived reformist government gave way to a series of governments that were dominated behind the scenes by military leader Fulgencio Batista until he was elected president in 1940. Batista was voted out of office in 1944 and was followed by two successive presidents in a democratic era that ultimately became characterized by corruption and increasing political violence. Batista seized power in a bloodless coup in 1952, and his rule progressed into a brutal dictatorship. This fueled popular unrest and set the stage for Fidel Castro's rise to power.

Castro led an unsuccessful attack on military barracks in Santiago, Cuba, on July 26, 1953. He was jailed, but subsequently freed and went into exile in Mexico, where he formed the 26th of July Movement. Castro returned to Cuba in 1956 with the goal of overthrowing the Batista dictatorship. His revolutionary movement was based in the Sierra Maestra mountains in eastern Cuba and joined with other resistance groups seeking Batista's ouster. Batista ultimately fled the country on January 1, 1959, leading to more than 45 years of rule under Fidel Castro until he stepped down from power provisionally in July 2006 because of poor health.

While Castro had promised a return to democratic constitutional rule when he first took power, he instead moved to consolidate his rule, repress dissent, and imprison or execute thousands of opponents. Under the new revolutionary government, Castro's supporters gradually displaced members of less radical groups. Castro moved toward close relations with the Soviet Union while relations with the United States deteriorated rapidly as the Cuban government expropriated U.S. properties. In April 1961, Castro declared that the Cuban revolution was socialist, and in December 1961, he proclaimed himself to be a Marxist-Leninist. Over the next 30 years, Cuba was a close ally of the Soviet Union and depended on it for significant assistance until the dissolution of the Soviet Union in 1991.

From 1959 until 1976, Castro ruled by decree. In 1976, however, the Cuban government enacted a new Constitution setting forth the Cuban Communist Party (PCC) as the leading force in state and society, with power centered in a Political Bureau headed by Fidel Castro. Cuba's Constitution also outlined national, provincial, and local governmental structures. Since then, legislative authority has been vested in a National Assembly of People's Power that meets twice annually for brief periods. When the Assembly is not in session, a Council of State, elected by the Assembly, acts on its behalf. According to Cuba's Constitution, the president of the Council of State is the country's head of state and government. Executive power in Cuba is vested in a Council of Ministers, also headed by the country's head of state and government, that is, the president of the Council of State.

Fidel Castro served as head of state and government through his position as president of the Council of State from 1976 until February 2008. While he had provisionally stepped down from power in July 2006 because of poor health, Fidel still officially retained his position as head of state and government. National Assembly elections were held in January 2008, and Fidel Castro was once again among the candidates elected to the 614-member legislative body. (As in the past, voters were offered a single slate of candidates.) On February 24, 2008, the new Assembly was scheduled to select from among its ranks the members of the Council of State and its president. Many observers had speculated that because of his poor health, Fidel would choose not to be reelected as president of the Council of State, which would confirm his official departure from heading the Cuban government. Statements from Castro himself in December 2007 hinted at his potential retirement. That proved true on February 19, 2008, when Fidel announced that he would not accept the position as president of the Council of State, essentially confirming his departure as titular head of the Cuban government.

Political Conditions

After Fidel stepped down from power, Cuba's political succession from Fidel to Raúl Castro was characterized by considerable stability. After two and a half years of provisionally serving as president, Raúl Castro officially became Cuba's president in February 2008, when Cuba's legislature selected him as president of the 31-member Council of State.[3] While Raúl Castro began implementing economic reforms in 2008, there has been no change to his government's tight control over the political system, and few observers expect such changes to occur with the government backed up by a strong security apparatus.

The Cuban Communist Party (PCC) held its sixth congress in April 2011. While the party concentrated on making changes to Cuba's economic model, some political changes also occurred. As expected, Raúl became first secretary of the PCC, officially replacing his brother Fidel. The party's Political Bureau or Politburo was reduced from 23 to 15 members, with 3 new members. The party's Central Committee also was reduced from 125 to 115 members, with about 80 of those being new members of the committee. Most significantly, Raúl Castro proposed two five-year term limits for top positions in the party and in the government, calling for systematic rejuvenation, a change that was confirmed by a January 2012 national PCC conference. Also at the 2012 conference, the PCC approved a resolution by which its Central Committee would be allowed to replace up to 20% of its 115 members within its five-year mandate.[4]

In February 2013, Cuba held elections for over 600 members of the National Assembly of People's Power, the national legislature, as well as over 1,600 provincial government representatives, both for five-year terms. Under Cuba's one-party system, the overwhelming majority of officials elected are PCC members. Critics maintain that elections in Cuba are a sham and entirely controlled by the PCC. The new National Assembly selected Raúl Castro for a second five-year term as president of the Council of State (Cuba's head of government). In conformity with the new two-term limit for top officials, Castro indicated that this would be his last term, which means that he would serve until February 2018, when he would be 86 years old.

Most significantly, a much younger official, Miguel Díaz-Canel Bermúdez (currently age 54), was selected to serve as first vice president of the Council of State, replacing 82-year José Ramón Machado, part of the older generation of so-called *históricos* of the 1959 Cuban revolution. The position of first vice president is significant because, according to the Cuban Constitution, the person holding the office is the official successor to the president. Prior to his appointment, DíazCanel—an engineer by training—was serving as one of the Council of State's six other vice presidents. His appointment as the official constitutional successor to Castro represents a move toward bringing about generational change in Cuba's political system. Díaz-Canel became a member of the Politburo in 2003 and also held top PCC positions in the provinces of Villa Clara and Holguín. He became education minister in 2009 until he was tapped to be a vice president of the Council of State. Díaz-Canel has been described in media reports as an experienced manager with good relations with the military and as someone that worked his way up through the party.[5]

Some Cuba watchers maintain that Díaz-Canel is still very much in the shadow of Raúl, and has not yet taken on a prominent role, and contend that the Cuban military is perhaps the most important institution to watch as the transition to a post-Castro government unfolds.[6] Under Raúl, who served as defense minister from the beginning of the Cuban revolution until 2008, the Cuban military has played an increasing role in government, with several military officers and confidants of Raúl serving as ministers.

In another significant move in February 2013, the National Assembly appointed Esteban Lazo Hernández as the new president of Cuba's National

Assembly. Lazo, who is the Cuban government's highest ranking official of Afro-Cuban descent, replaced long-time National Assembly President Ricardo Alarcón. Lazo previously held top party positions in several provinces and had served as a vice president of the Council of State.

While generational change already appears to be underway in Cuba's political system, this does not signify an easing of Cuba's tightly controlled regime. Speaking on the 60th anniversary of the start of the Cuban revolution on July 26, 2013, President Castro asserted that a generational transfer of power had already begun, stating that "there is a slow and orderly transfer of the leadership of the revolution to the new generations."[7] While the leadership transition due in 2018 is set to be smooth, there is also greater likelihood for a growth in factionalism within the system without Castro at the helm.

Human Rights

The Cuban government has a poor record on human rights, with the government sharply restricting freedoms of expression, association, assembly, movement, and other basic rights since the early years of the Cuban revolution. The government has continued to harass members of the Ladies in White (*Damas de Blanco*) human rights group that was formed in 2003 by the female relatives of the so-called "group of 75" dissidents arrested that year in a massive crackdown (for more, see text box below). Two Cuban political prisoners conducting hunger strikes have died in recent years, Orlando Zapata Tamayo in February 2010 and Wilman Villar Mendoza in January 2012. Tamayo died after an 85-day hunger strike that he had initiated to protest inhumane conditions in Cuba's prisons. Villar Mendoza died following a 50-day hunger strike after he was convicted of "contempt" of authority and sentenced to four years in prison.

Amnesty International (AI) published a report in March 2012 maintaining that "the Cuban government wages a permanent campaign of harassment and short-term detentions of political opponents to stop them from demanding respect for civil and political rights." The report maintained that the release of dozens of political prisoners in 2011 "did not herald a change in human rights policy." AI asserted that "the vast majority of those released were forced into exile, while in Cuba the authorities were determined to contain the dissidence and government critics with new tactics," including intimidation, harassment, surveillance, and "acts of repudiation," or demonstrations by government supporters targeting government critics.[8]

In 2013, AI had named five jailed dissidents "prisoners of conscience"[9] in Cuba. All five were released in early January 2015 as part of the Cuban government's release of 53 political prisoners that was announced in December 2014. Two of the five, Emilio Planas Robert and Iván Fernández Depestre, were released without restriction. They had been imprisoned since September 2012 and July 2013, respectively, and had been convicted of "dangerousness" (a preemptive measure defined as the special proclivity of a person to commit crimes). The other three "prisoners of conscience," brothers Alexeis, Django, and Vianco Vargas Martín, were released conditionally and need to report regularly to local authorities. All three were members of the Patriotic Union of Cuba (UNPACU), a dissident organization, and were detained in late 2012 and convicted in June 2014 after a summary trial in which they were charged with "public disorder."[10] Three other dissidents whose cases were followed by AI were released from prison on December 9, 2014—Ladies in White member Sonia Garro Alfonso; her husband, Ramón Alejandro Muñoz González; and a neighbor, Eugenio Hernández. They had been held since March 2012 without trial and were reportedly placed under house arrest awaiting trial when released in December.[11]

Going beyond AI's narrow definition of prisoners of conscience, the Cuban government has held a larger number of political prisoners, generally defined as a person imprisoned for his or her political activities. While the Cuban government released numerous political prisoners in recent years, including more than 125 released in 2010-2011 with the help of Cuba's Catholic Church (down from more than 200 estimated at the beginning of 2010), the number of political prisoners reportedly increased beginning in 2012, according to the Havana-based Cuban Commission on Human Rights and National Reconciliation (CCDHRN). In June 2014, the group estimated that Cuba held at least 102 political prisoners, not including a dozen individuals arrested in Cuba's 2003 crackdown that were released on parole, but are prevented from leaving the country.[12]

As noted above, Cuba released 53 political prisoners in the aftermath of the most recent U.S. policy change toward Cuba; reportedly 17 had been released before the announcement and the remainder by January 12, 2015.[13] The list of 53 prisoners had been drawn up by the Obama Administration and included only those jailed for having peacefully exercised their rights of freedom of expression and assembly.[14] The CCDHRN list of political prisoners from 2014 included 52 of the 53 political prisoners released.[15]

Short-term detentions for political reasons have increased significantly over the past several years, a reflection of the government's change of tactics in repressing dissent away from longterm imprisonment. The CCDHRN reports that there were at least 2,074 such detentions in 2010, 4,123 in 2011,

6,602 in 2012, and 6,424 in 2013. For 2014, the group reported that there were 8,899 such detentions, almost 39% higher than the previous year. In January 2015, the number of short-term detentions was 178, which is the lowest level for the same period since 2010, according to the CCDHRN.[16] Nevertheless, it is too early to discern whether there is a downward trend in detentions.

Over the past several years, numerous independent Cuban blogs have been established that are often critical of the Cuban government. Cuban blogger Yoani Sánchez has received considerable international attention since 2007 for her website, Generación Y, which includes commentary critical of the Cuban government.[17] In May 2014, Sánchez launched an independent digital newspaper in Cuba, available on the Internet, distributed through a variety of methods in Cuba, including CDs, USB flash drives, and DVDs.[18]

While the human rights situation in Cuba remains poor, the country has made some advances in recent years. In 2008, Cuba lifted a ban on Cubans staying in hotels that previously had been restricted to foreign tourists in a policy that had been pejoratively referred to as "tourist apartheid." In recent years, as the government has enacted limited economic reforms, it has been much more open to debate on economic issues. The Catholic Church, which played a prominent role in the release of political prisoners in 2010, has been active in broadening the debate on social and economic issues through its publications *Palabra Nueva* (New Word) and *Espacio Laical* (Space for Laity).[19] In June 2014, the two editors of *Espacio Laical*, Roberto Veiga and Lenier Gonzalez, resigned from their positions, maintaining that they had been pressured from inside the Church from those who did not want the Church to be involved in politics, but they announced soon after the launch of an online forum known as *Cuba Posible*.[20] In January 2013, Cuba took the significant step of eliminating its long-standing policy of requiring an exit permit and letter of invitation for Cubans to travel abroad. The change has allowed prominent dissidents and human rights activists to travel abroad and return to Cuba. However, those Cubans subject to ongoing legal proceedings, including political prisoners who have been released on parole, have been restricted from traveling abroad.[21]

In June 2014, the State Department released its 2014 Trafficking in Persons Report. As it has since 2003, Cuba remained on the Tier 3 list of countries whose governments do not comply with the minimum standards for combatting trafficking against Cuba. The report noted, however, that for the first time Cuba reported concrete action against sex trafficking, and that the Cuban government maintained that it would be amending its criminal code to ensure conformity with the 2000 United Nations Trafficking in Persons Protocol.

Human Rights Reporting on Cuba

Amnesty International (AI), Human Rights in the Republic of Cuba, http://www.amnesty.org/en/region/cuba.

AI, "Routine Repression, Political Short-Term Detentions and Harassment in Cuba," March 2012, available at http://www.amnesty.org/en/library/asset/AMR25/007/2012/en/647943e7-b4eb-4d39-a5e3-ea061edb651c/amr250072012en.pdf.

Cuban Commission on Human Rights and National Reconciliation (Comisión Cubana de Derechos Humanos y Reconciliación Nacional, CCDHRN), the independent Havana-based human rights organization produces a monthly report on short-term detentions for political reasons.

CCDHRN, "Cuba: Algunos Actos de Represion Politica en el Mes de Enero de 2015," February 2, 2015, available at http://www.14ymedio.com/nacional/CCDHRN-enero-2015_CYMFIL20150202_0001.pdf;

CCDHRN, "Lisa Parcial de Condenados o Procesados por Motivos Politicos en Cuba," June 23, 2014, available at http://www.unpacu.org/wp-content/uploads/PRESOS-POLITICOS-JUNIO-2014.pdf;

14ymedio.com, independent digital newspaper, based in Havana available at http://www.14ymedio.com/.

Human Rights Watch (HRW), http://www.hrw.org/en/americas/cuba.

HRW's 2015 World Report maintains that "the Cuban government continues to repress individuals and groups who criticize the government or call for basic human rights," available at http://www.hrw.org/sites/default/files/reports/wr2015_web.pdf (pp. 181-186).

Inter-American Commission on Human Rights, Annual Report 2013, April 23, 2014, Chapter IV has a section on Cuba, available at: http://www.oas.org/en/iachr/docs/annual/2013/docs-en/AnnualReport-Chap4-Cuba.pdf.

U.S. Department of State, Country Report on Human Rights Practices for 2013, February 27, 2014, available at http://www.state./organization/220646.pdf.

Economic Conditions

Cuba's economy is largely state-controlled, with the government owning most means of production and employing a majority of the workforce. Key sectors of the economy that generate foreign exchange include the export of professional services (largely medical personnel to Venezuela); tourism, which has grown significantly since the mid-1990s, with 2.8 million tourists visiting Cuba in 2013 (below a goal of 3 million tourists); nickel mining, with the Canadian mining company Sherritt International involved in a joint investment project; and a biotechnology and pharmaceutical sector that supplies the domestic healthcare system and has fostered a significant export industry. Remittances from relatives living abroad, especially from the United States, have also become an important source of hard currency. The once-dominant sugar industry has declined significantly over the past 20 years; in 1990, Cuba produced 8.4 million tons of sugar, while in 2014 it produced 1.6 million tons.[22]

Cuba is highly dependent on Venezuela for its oil needs. In 2000, the two countries signed a preferential oil agreement that provides Cuba with some 100,000 barrels of oil per day, about two-thirds of its consumption. Cuba's goal of becoming a net oil exporter with the development of its offshore deepwater oil reserves was set back significantly in 2012, when the drilling of three exploratory oil wells was unsuccessful. The setback in Cuba's offshore oil development combined with political and economic difficulties in Venezuela have raised concerns among Cuban officials about the security of the support received from Venezuela. Cuba is increasingly focusing on the need to diversify its trading partners and to seek alternative energy suppliers in the case of a cutback or cutoff of Venezuelan oil.[23]

Over the years, Cuba has expressed pride for the nation's accomplishments in health and education. According to the United Nations Development Program's 2014 Human Development Report, Cuba is ranked 44 out of 187 countries worldwide and is characterized as having "very high human development," with life expectancy in Cuba in 2013 at 79.3 years and adult literacy estimated at almost 100%.

In terms of economic growth, Cuba experienced severe economic deterioration from 1989 to 1993, with an estimated decline in gross domestic product ranging from 35% to 50% when the Soviet Union collapsed and Russian financial assistance to Cuba practically ended. Since then, however, there has been considerable improvement. From 1994 to 2000, as Cuba moved forward with some limited market-oriented economic reforms, economic growth averaged 3.7% annually. Economic growth was especially strong in the 2004-2007 period, registering an impressive 11% and 12%, respectively, in 2005 and 2006 (see **Figure 2**). The economy benefitted from the growth of the tourism, nickel, and oil sectors and support from Venezuela and China in terms of investment commitments and credit lines. However, the economy was hard hit by several hurricanes and storms in 2008 and the global financial crisis in 2009, with the government having to implement austerity measures. As a result, economic growth slowed significantly.

Since 2010, growth has improved modestly, with 2.4% growth in 2010, 2.8% in 2011, 3% in 2012, and 2.7% in 2013, according to the Economist Intelligence Unit (EIU). In 2014, the estimate is 1.3% growth, downgraded from EIU's original forecast of 2.1% growth because of Cuba's challenges in shifting from a centrally planned to a more decentralized economy. The EIU projects stronger growth rates averaging over 5% in the 2015-2019 period but notes that the withdrawal of support from Venezuela could jeopardize these forecasts.[24] Some economists maintain that Cuba needs a growth rate of at least 5% to 7% in order to develop the economy and create new jobs—increasing internal savings and attracting foreign investment reportedly are keys to achieving such growth rates.[25]

The government of Raúl Castro has implemented a number of economic policy changes, but there has been some disappointment that more far-reaching reforms have not been forthcoming. As noted above, the government employs a majority of the labor force, almost 80%, but it has been allowing more private sector activities. In 2010, the government opened up a wide range of activities for self-employment and small businesses. There are now almost 200 categories of work allowed, and the number of self-employed has risen from some 156,000 at the end of 2010 to some 500,000 at the end of 2014 out of a workforce of over 5 million.[26]

Analysts contend, however, that the government needs to do more to support the development of the private sector, including an expansion of authorized activities to include more white-collar occupations and state support for credit to support small businesses. A major challenge for the development of the private sector is the lack of money in circulation. Most Cubans do not make enough money to support the development of small businesses; those private sector activities catering to tourists and foreign diplomats have fared better than those serving the Cuban market. The government's decisions in 2013 to crack down on privately run movie and video game salons and on private sales of imported clothes and hardware raised questions about its commitment to the development of the private sector. In December 2013, Raúl Castro issued a warning against those engaging in economic activities not strictly authorized by the state, maintaining that it creates an environment of impunity.[27]

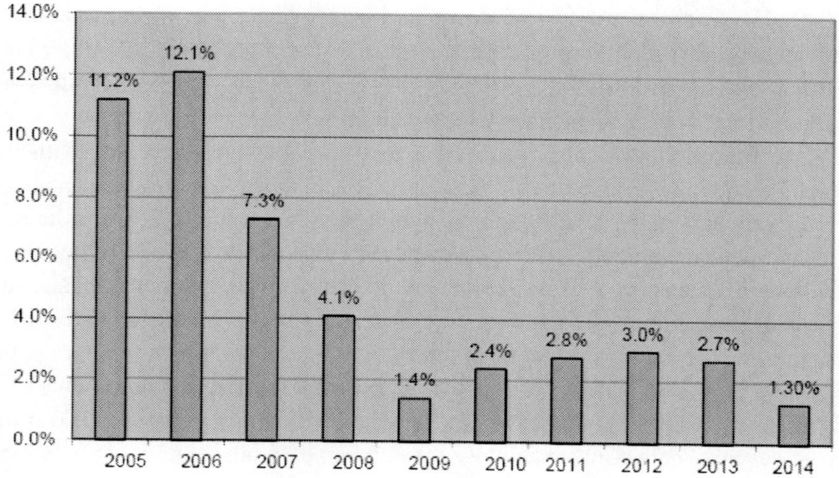

Source: Economist Intelligence Unit, Country Data Tool, 2015.

Figure 2. Cuba: Real GDP Growth (%), 2005-2014.

Among Cuba's significant economic challenges are low wages (whereby workers cannot satisfy basic human needs) and the related problem of how to unify Cuba's two official currencies circulating in the country.[28] Most people are paid in Cuban pesos (CUPs), and the minimum monthly wage in Cuba is about 225 pesos (about U.S. $9),[29] but for increasing amounts of consumer goods, convertible pesos (CUCs) are used. (For personal transactions, the exchange rate for the two currencies is CUP24/CUC1.) Cubans with access to foreign remittances or who work in jobs that give them access to convertible pesos are far better off than those Cubans who do not have such access.

In October 2013, the Cuban government announced that it would move toward ending its dual-currency system and move toward monetary unification. In March 2014, the government provided insight about how monetary unification would move forward when it published instructions for when the CUC is removed from circulation; no date was provided, but it was referred to as "day zero." There is significant uncertainty about the actual date and the details of the exchange rate system that would replace it.[30] Currency reform is ultimately expected to lead to productivity gains and improve the business climate, but an adjustment would create winners and losers.[31]

A significant reform effort under Raúl Castro has focused on the agricultural sector, a vital issue because Cuba imports some 60% of its food needs. In an effort to boost food production, the government has turned over idle land to farmers and given farmers more control over how to use their land and what supplies to buy. Despite these and other efforts, overall food production has been significantly below targets.

In March 2014, Cuba approved a new foreign investment law with the goal of attracting needed foreign capital to the country. The law cuts taxes on profits by half, to 15%, and exempts companies from paying taxes for the first eight years of operation. Employment or labor taxes are also eliminated, although companies still must hire labor through state-run companies, with agreed-upon wages. A fast-track procedure for small projects reportedly will streamline the approval process, and the government has agreed to improve the transparency and time of the approval process for larger investments.[32] It remains to be seen to what extent the new law will attract investment. Over the past several years, Cuba has closed a number of joint ventures with foreign companies and has arrested several executives of foreign companies reportedly for corrupt practices. According to some observers, investors will want evidence, not just legislation, that the government is prepared to allow foreign investors to make a profit in Cuba.[33]

In October 2014, the Cuban government issued a list of some 246 projects in which it was seeking some $8.7 billion in investment in such sectors as energy, tourism, agriculture, and industry.[34]

A number of Cuba's economists are pressing for the government to enact more far-reaching reforms and embrace competition for key parts of the economy and state-run enterprises. They criticize the government's continued reliance on central planning and its monopoly in foreign trade.[35]

For Additional Reading on the Cuban Economy

Association for the Study of the Cuban Economy, annual proceedings, available at http://www.ascecuba.org/publications/annual-proceedings/.

Brookings Institution, webpage on Cuba,
http://www.brookings.edu/research/topics/cuba;

Richard E. Feinberg and Ted Piccone, eds., *Cuba's Economic Change in Comparative Perspective*, November 2014, available at http://www.brookings.edu/research/papers/2014/11/cuba-economic-change-comparative-perspective;

Ted Piccone and Harold Trinkunas, *The Cuba-Venezuela Alliance: The Beginning of the End?* June 2004, available at http://www.brookings.edu/research/papers/2014/06/16-cuba-venezuela-alliance-piccone-trinkunas;

Philip Peters, *Cuba's New Real Estate Market*, February 2014, available at http://www.brookings.edu/research/reports/2014/02/21-cuba-real-estate-market-peters; and

Richard Feinberg, *Soft Landing in Cuba? Emerging Entrepreneurs and Middle Classes*, November 2013, available at http://www.brookings.edu/research/reports/2013/11/cuba-entrepreneurs-middle-classes-feinberg.

The Cuban Economy, La Economia Cubana, website maintained by Arch Ritter, from Carlton University, Ottawa, Canada, available at http://thecubaneconomy.com/.

Revista Temas (Havana), links to the Cuban journal's articles on economy and politics, in Spanish available at http://www.temas.cult.cu/catalejo.php.

Oficina Nacional de Estadísticas e Información, República de Cuba (Cuba's National Office of Statistics and Information), available at http://www.one.cu/.

Cuba's Foreign Relations

During the Cold War, Cuba had extensive relations with and support from the Soviet Union, with billions of dollars in annual subsidies to sustain the Cuban economy. This subsidy system helped fund an activist foreign policy and support for guerrilla movements and revolutionary governments abroad in Latin America and Africa. With an end to the Cold War, the dissolution of the Soviet Union, and the loss of Soviet financial support, Cuba was forced to abandon its revolutionary activities abroad. As its economy reeled from the loss of Soviet support, Cuba was forced to open up its economy and economic relations with countries worldwide. In 2013, Cuba's leading trading partners in terms of Cuban exports were Venezuela (almost 43%), Canada, the Netherlands, and China, while the leading sources of Cuba's imports were Venezuela (almost 33%), China, Spain, Brazil, Mexico, Italy, Canada, and the United States (2.7%).[36]

Russia

Relations with Russia, which had diminished significantly in the aftermath of the Cold War, have been strengthened somewhat over the past several years. In 2008, then-Russian President Dmitry Medvedev visited Havana, while Raúl Castro visited Russia in 2009 and again in 2012. Current Russian President Vladimir Putin visited Cuba in July 2014 on his way to attend the BRICS[37] summit in Brazil. Just before arriving in Cuba, Putin signed into law an agreement writing off 90% of Cuba's $32 billion Soviet-era debt, with some $3.5 billion to be paid back by Cuba over a 10-year period that would fund Russian investment projects in Cuba.[38] In the aftermath of Putin's trip, there were press reports alleging that Russia would reopen its signals intelligence facility at Lourdes, Cuba, which had closed in 2002, but President Putin denied reports that his government would reopen the facility.[39]

While trade relations between Russia and Cuba are not significant, two Russian energy companies have been involved in oil exploration in Cuba, and a third announced its involvement in 2014. Gazprom had been in a partnership with the Malaysian state oil company, Petronas, that conducted unsuccessful deepwater oil drilling off of Cuba's western coast in 2012. The Russian oil company Zarubezhneft began drilling in Cuba's shallow coastal waters east of Havana in December 2012, but stopped work in April 2013 because of disappointing results. During President Putin's July 2014 visit to Cuba, Russian energy companies Rosneft and Zarubezhneft signed an agreement with Cuba's state oil company CubaPetroleo (Cupet) for the development of an offshore exploration block, and Rosneft agreed to cooperate with Cuba in studying ways to optimize existing production at mature fields.[40] Some energy analysts are skeptical about the prospects for the offshore project given the unsuccessful attempts by foreign oil companies drilling wells in Cuba's deepwaters.

China

Relations with China have also strengthened in recent years. During the Cold War, the two countries did not have close relations because of Sino-Soviet tensions, but bilateral relations have grown close in recent years, with Chinese trade and investment in Cuba increasing. Chinese President Hu Jintao visited Cuba in 2004 and again in 2008, while Chinese Vice President Xi Jinping visited Cuba in June 2011 and again in July 2014, this time as China's president, after attending the BRICS summit in Brazil. Raúl Castro had also visited China in 2012 on a four-day visit, in which the two countries reportedly signed cooperation agreements focusing on trade and investment issues.

During Xi Jinping's 2014 visit, the two countries reportedly signed 29 trade, debt, credit, and other agreements. While in Cuba, the Chinese president said that "China and Cuba being socialist countries, we are closely united by the same missions, ideals, and struggles."[41]

European Union

The European Union (EU) and Cuba held two rounds of talks in 2014—in April and August—on a framework agreement for cooperation covering political, trade, and development issues, and reports indicate that the two sides have made significant progress; a third round is to take place in early March 2015.[42] In 1996, the EU adopted a Common Position on Cuba, stating that the objective of EU relations with Cuba includes encouraging "a process of transition to pluralist democracy and respect for human rights and fundamental freedoms." The position also stipulated that full EU economic cooperation with Cuba would depend upon improvements in human rights and political freedom.[43]

Venezuela and Other Latin American Countries

For almost 15 years, Venezuela has been a significant source of support for Cuba. Dating back to 2000 under populist President Hugo Chávez, Venezuela began providing subsidized oil (some 100,000 barrels per day) and investment. For its part, Cuba has sent thousands of medical personnel to Venezuela. In the aftermath of Chávez's death in March 2013, the close Venezuelan presidential election in April 2013 won by Nicolás Maduro of the ruling Socialist party, and Venezuela's mounting economic challenges since mid-2014 because of the rapid decline in oil prices, Cuban officials are reportedly concerned about the future of Venezuelan support.

With El Salvador's restoration of relations with Cuba in June 2009, all Latin American nations now have official diplomatic relations with Cuba. Cuba has increasingly become more engaged in Latin America beyond the already close relations with Venezuela. Cuba is a member of the Bolivarian Alliance for the Americas (ALBA), a Venezuelan-led integration and cooperation scheme founded in 2004. In August 2013, Cuba began deploying thousands of doctors to Brazil in a program aimed at providing doctors to rural areas of Brazil, with Cuba earning some $225 million a year for supplying the medical personnel.[44] Brazil also has been a major investor in the development of the port of Mariel west of Havana.

Community of Latin American and Caribbean States (CELAC)

Cuba became a full member of the Rio Group of Latin American and Caribbean nations in November 2008, and a member of the succeeding CELAC that was officially established in December 2011 to boost regional cooperation, but without the participation of the United States or Canada. In January 2013, Raúl Castro assumed the presidency of the organization for one year, and Cuba hosted the group's second summit in January 2014 in Havana, attended by leaders from across the hemisphere as well as United Nations Secretary General Ban Ki-moon and Organization of American States (OAS) Secretary General José Miguel Insulza. The U.N. Secretary General reportedly raised human rights issues with Cuban officials, including the subject of Cuba's ratification of U.N. human rights accords and "arbitrary detentions" by the Cuban government.[45]

Summit of the Americas

Cuba had expressed interest in attending the sixth Summit of the Americas in April 2012 in Cartagena, Colombia, but ultimately was not invited to attend. The United States and Canada expressed opposition to Cuba's participation. Previous summits have been limited to the hemisphere's 34 democratically elected leaders, and the OAS (in which Cuba does not participate) has played a key role in summit implementation and follow-up activities. Several Latin American nations vowed not to attend the next Summit of the Americas to be held in Panama in April 2015 unless Cuba was allowed to participate, and as a result, Panama announced in August 2014 that it would invite Cuba to attend. Cuba's participation was a looming challenge for the Obama Administration, but in December 2014, when President Obama announced a new policy approach toward Cuba, he said that the United States was prepared to have Cuba participate in the summit.

OAS

Cuba was excluded from participation in the OAS in 1962 because of its identification with Marxism-Leninism, but in 2009, the OAS overturned the 1962 resolution in a move that could eventually lead to Cuba's reentry into the regional organization in accordance with the practices, purposes, and principles of the OAS. While the Cuban government welcomed the OAS vote to overturn the 1962 resolution, it asserted that it would not return to the OAS.[46]

International Organizations

Cuba is an active participant in international forums, including the United Nations and the controversial United Nations Human Rights Council. Since 1991, the U.N. General Assembly has approved a resolution each year criticizing the U.S. economic embargo and urging the United States to lift it. Cuba also has received support over the years from the United Nations Development Programme (UNDP) and the United Nations Educational, Scientific, and Cultural Organization (UNESCO), both of which have offices in Havana. The U.N. has played a significant role in providing relief and recovery from Hurricane Sandy that struck in October 2012. Among other international organizations, Cuba was a founding member of the World Trade Organization, but it is not a member of the International Monetary Fund, the World Bank, or the Inter-American Development Bank.

Compliance with U.N. Sanctions on North Korea

In July 2013, the discovery of a weapons shipment aboard a North Korean ship that had left Cuba on its way back to North Korea raised questions about the nature of Cuban-North Korean relations and about Cuba's compliance with U.N. sanctions against North Korea. Panama had detained the North Korean ship as it prepared to enter the Panama Canal due to suspicion that the ship was carrying illicit narcotics; instead, the ship was found to be carrying military weapons. The U.N. Security Council's Panel of Experts for North Korea visited Panama in August 2013 and issued a report on the incident in March 2014. The Panel of Experts concluded that both the shipment and the transaction between Cuba and North Korea were violations of U.N. sanctions banning weapons transfers to North Korea.[47] In July 2014, the U.N. Security Council imposed sanctions on the operator of the North Korean ship, and the company is now subject to an international asset freeze.[48] U.S. Ambassador to the United Nations Samantha Power described the North Korean ship incident as a "cynical, outrageous and illegal attempt by Cuba and North Korea to circumvent United Nations sanctions."[49]

U.S. Policy Toward Cuba

Background on U.S.-Cuban Relations[50]

In the early 1960s, U.S.-Cuban relations deteriorated sharply when Fidel Castro began to build a repressive communist dictatorship and moved his country toward close relations with the Soviet Union. The often tense and hostile nature of the U.S.-Cuban relationship is illustrated by such events and actions as U.S. covert operations to overthrow the Castro government culminating in the ill-fated April 1961 Bay of Pigs invasion; the October 1962 missile crisis in which the United States confronted the Soviet Union over its attempt to place offensive nuclear missiles in Cuba; Cuban support for guerrilla insurgencies and military support for revolutionary governments in Africa and the Western Hemisphere; the 1980 exodus of around 125,000 Cubans to the United States in the so-called Mariel boatlift; the 1994 exodus of more than 30,000 Cubans who were interdicted and housed at U.S. facilities in Guantanamo and Panama; and the 1996 shootdown by Cuban fighter jets of two U.S. civilian planes operated by the Cuban-American group Brothers to the Rescue, which resulted in the deaths of four U.S. crew members.

Since the early 1960s, U.S. policy toward Cuba has consisted largely of isolating the island nation through comprehensive economic sanctions, including an embargo on trade and financial transactions. President Kennedy proclaimed an embargo on trade between the United States and Cuba in February 1962,[51] citing Section 620(a) of the Foreign Assistance Act of 1961 (FAA), which authorizes the President "to establish and maintain a total embargo upon all trade between the United States and Cuba."[52] At the same time, the Department of the Treasury issued the Cuban Import Regulations to deny the importation into the United States of all goods imported from or through Cuba.[53] The authority for the embargo was later expanded in March 1962 to include the Trading with the Enemy Act (TWEA).[54]

In July 1963, the Treasury Department revoked the Cuban Import Regulations and replaced them with the more comprehensive Cuban Assets Control Regulations (CACR)—31 C.F.R. Part 515— under the authority of TWEA and Section 620(a) of the FAA.[55] The CACR, which include a prohibition on most financial transactions with Cuba and a freeze of Cuban government assets in the United States, remain the main body of Cuba embargo regulations and have been amended many times over the years to reflect changes in policy. They are administered by the Treasury Department's Office of Foreign Assets Control (OFAC) and prohibit financial transactions as well as trade transactions with Cuba. The CACR also require that all exports to Cuba be licensed by the Department of Commerce, Bureau of Industry and Security, under the provisions of the Export Administration Act of 1979, as amended.[56] The Export Administration Regulations (EAR) are found at 15 C.F.R. Sections 730-774.[57]

Congress subsequently strengthened sanctions on Cuba with enactment of the Cuban Democracy Act (CDA) of 1992 (P.L. 102-484, Title XVII), the Cuban Liberty and Democratic Solidarity (LIBERTAD) Act of 1996 (P.L. 104-114), and the Trade Sanctions Reform and Export Enhancement Act of 2000 (P.L. 106-387, Title IX).

- Among its provisions, the CDA prohibits U.S. foreign subsidiaries from engaging in trade with Cuba and prohibits entry into the United States for any sea-borne vessel to load or unload freight if it has been involved in trade with Cuba within the previous 180 days.
- The LIBERTAD Act, enacted in the aftermath of Cuba's shooting down of two U.S. civilian planes in February 1996, combines a variety of measures to increase pressure on Cuba and provides for a plan to assist Cuba once it begins the transition to democracy. Most significantly, the law codified the Cuban embargo, including all restrictions under the CACR. This provision is noteworthy because of its long-lasting effect on U.S. policy options toward Cuba. The executive branch is prevented from lifting the economic embargo without congressional concurrence until certain democratic conditions set forth in the law are met, although the President retains broad authority to amend the regulations therein. Another significant sanction in Title III of the law holds any person or government that traffics in U.S. property confiscated by the Cuban government liable for monetary damages in U.S. federal court. Acting under provisions of the law, however, Presidents Clinton, Bush, and Obama have suspended the implementation of Title III at six-month intervals.
- While TSRA authorizes U.S. commercial exports to Cuba, it also includes prohibitions on U.S. assistance and financing and requires "payment of cash in advance" or third-country financing for the exports. The act also prohibits tourist travel to Cuba.

In addition to these acts, Congress enacted numerous other provisions of law over the years that impose sanctions on Cuba, including restrictions on trade, foreign aid, and support from international financial institutions. The government of Cuba also was designated by the State Department as a state sponsor of international terrorism in 1982 under Section 6(j) of the Export Administration Act and other laws because of its alleged ties to international terrorism.[58]

In addition to sanctions, another component of U.S. policy has consisted of support measures for the Cuban people. This includes U.S. private humanitarian donations, medical exports to Cuba under the terms of the CDA, U.S. government support for democracy-building efforts, and U.S.- sponsored radio and television broadcasting to Cuba. The enactment of TSRA by the 106th

Congress also led to the United States becoming one of Cuba's largest suppliers of agricultural products. Authorization for purposeful travel to Cuba and cash remittances to Cuba have constituted important means to support the Cuban people, although there has been significant congressional debate over these issues for many years.

Despite the poor state of U.S.-Cuban relations, there have been several examples of bilateral cooperation over the years in areas of shared national interest. Three areas that stand out are alien migrant interdiction (with migration accords negotiated in 1994 and 1995), counternarcotics cooperation (with increased cooperation dating back to 1999), and cooperation on oil spill preparedness and prevention (since 2011).

Obama Administration Policy

During its first six years, the Obama Administration continued the dual-track policy approach toward Cuba that has been in place for many years. It maintained U.S. economic sanctions and continued measures to support the Cuban people, such as U.S. government-sponsored radio and television broadcasting and funding for democracy and human rights projects.

At the same time, however, the Obama Administration initiated a significant shift in policy toward Cuba beginning in 2009. As part of the policy of reaching out to the Cuban people, President Obama fulfilled a campaign pledge by lifting all restrictions on family travel and remittances. At the April 2009 Summit of the Americas, President Obama announced that "the United States seeks a new beginning with Cuba." While recognizing that it would take time to "overcome decades of mistrust," the President said "there are critical steps we can take toward a new day." He stated that he was prepared to have his Administration "engage with the Cuban government on a wide range of issues—from drugs, migration, and economic issues, to human rights, free speech, and democratic reform."[59] In the aftermath of the Summit in 2009, there was some momentum toward improved relations: in July, the two countries restarted semiannual migration talks that had been suspended by the

United States five years earlier; in September, the two countries held talks on resuming direct mail service.

Alan Gross Case

U.S.-Cuban relations took a turn for the worse in December 2009 when Alan Gross, an American subcontractor working on Cuba democracy projects funded by the U.S. Agency for International Development (USAID) was arrested in Havana. Gross was providing Internet communications equipment to Cuba's Jewish community. He was convicted in March 2011 on charges of acting "against the independence and territorial integrity of the state," and sentenced to 15 years in prison. U.S. officials and some Members of Congress repeatedly raised the issue with the Cuban government and asked for his release. In the aftermath of Gross's conviction, the United States and Cuba continued to cooperate on issues of shared national interest, such as antidrug efforts and migration interdiction, but improvement of relations in other areas became stymied. Securing his release remained a top U.S. priority until he was ultimately released by the Cuban government on December 17, 2014.

The Obama Administration introduced new measures in 2011 to further reach out to the Cuban people through increased purposeful travel (including people-to-people educational travel) and an easing of restrictions on non-family remittances. Beginning in mid-2013, there was also renewed engagement with Cuba on several fronts, including direct mail service talks, resumed migration talks (that had not taken place for 18 months), and air and maritime search and rescue.

In remarks made in November 2013 on policy toward Cuba, President Obama maintained that "we have to be creative ... we have to be thoughtful ... and we have to continue to update our policies." He contended that "the notion that the same policies that we put in place in 1961 would somehow still be as effective as they are today in the age of the Internet and Google and world travel doesn't make sense."[60]

Throughout the Obama Administration's first six years, human rights violations in Cuba remained a fundamental concern. President Obama and the State Department continued to issue statements expressing concern about violations as they occurred, including the death of hunger strikers in 2010 and 2012 and targeted repression against dissidents and human rights activists. As noted above, securing the release of Alan Gross from prison in Cuba also remained a top U.S. priority. The State Department maintained that it was using every appropriate channel to press for his release, including the Vatican.

President Obama Unveils a New Policy Approach Toward Cuba

On December 17, 2014, just after the adjournment of the 113th Congress, President Obama announced major developments in U.S.-Cuban relations and unveiled a new policy approach toward Cuba. First, he announced that the Cuban government had released Alan Gross on humanitarian grounds after five years of imprisonment. The President also announced that, in a separate action, the Cuban government released "one of the most important intelligence assets that the United States has ever had in Cuba" in exchange for three Cuban intelligence agents who had been imprisoned in the United States since 1998. Media reports identified the U.S. intelligence asset as Rolando Sarraff Trujillo, a cryptographer in Cuba's Directorate of Intelligence, who reportedly provided information that helped the FBI dismantle three Cuban spy networks in the United States.[61]

Most significantly, in the aftermath of having secured the release of Gross and the U.S. intelligence asset, President Obama announced a major shift in U.S. policy toward Cuba, moving away from a sanctions-based policy aimed at isolating Cuba to a policy of engagement. The President said that his Administration

> will end an outdated approach that, for decades, has failed to advance our interests, and instead we will begin to normalize relations between our two countries. Through these changes, we intend to create more opportunities for the American and Cuban people, and begin a new chapter among the nations of the Americas.

The President maintained that the United States would continue to raise concerns about democracy and human rights in Cuba but stated that "we can do more to support the Cuban people and promote our values through engagement." According to the President, "After all, these 50 years have shown that isolation has not worked. It's time for a new approach."[62]

The President outlined three major steps to move toward normalization: (1) the reestablishment of diplomatic relations with Cuba; (2) a review of Cuba's designation by the Department of State as a state sponsor of international terrorism; and (3) an increase in travel, commerce, and the flow of information to and from Cuba.

Reestablishment of Diplomatic Relations

As U.S.-Cuban relations deteriorated in the early 1960s, relations were severed by the Eisenhower Administration in January 1961 in response to the Cuban government's demand to decrease the number of U.S. Embassy staff within 48 hours. In 1977, under the Carter Administration, both countries established Interests Sections in each other's capitals.

Assistant Secretary of State for Western Hemisphere Affairs Roberta Jacobson visited Cuba January 21-24, 2015, for talks to start the process of normalizing relations, including the logistics of reopening embassies and embassy operations. The first day of talks focused on migration issues since the meeting originally was scheduled as a semi-annual discussion on the implementation of migration accords negotiated in 1994 and 1995. The second day of talks focused on the reestablishment of diplomatic relations.[63] The Cuban delegation was headed by Josefina Vidal, director of the North American division of Cuba's Ministry of Foreign Relations. Ahead of the talks, Jacobson maintained that the focus would be on allowing diplomats to have the full range of privileges and carry out their full range of roles as diplomats as in other countries.[64] Issues discussed reportedly included staffing numbers, lifting in-country travel restrictions on diplomats, unimpeded shipments for the diplomatic post, and access to the post by Cubans. According to the State Department, the U.S. Interests Section in Havana currently has a cap of 51 direct U.S. hires, a cap previously jointly agreed by the United States and Cuba.[65]

A second round of talks is scheduled for February 27, 2015, in Washington, DC, again led by Jacobson and Vidal. Ahead of those talks, a senior Cuban official called for the United States to remove Cuba from the state sponsors of terrorism list before the reestablishment of diplomatic relations.[66] U.S. officials, however, emphasize that the two processes—the reestablishment of relations and the terrorism review—are separate. Once diplomatic relations are established, the United States wants to have a number of substantive dialogues with the Cuban government on various issues. The first of these is likely to be on human rights, according to the State Department, with Assistant Secretary of State for Democracy, Human Rights, and Labor Tom Malinowski leading the U.S. side.[67]

Review of Cuba's Designation As a State Sponsor of International Terrorism

Cuba has been on the list since 1982 pursuant to Section 6(j) of the Export Administration Act (EAA) of 1979 (P.L. 96-72; 50 U.S.C. Appendix 2504(j)) and other laws because of its alleged ties to international terrorism and support for terrorist groups in Latin America. President Obama directed Secretary of State Kerry to review Cuba's designation "guided by the facts and the law." The President stated that "at a time when we are focused on threats from al Qaeda to ISIL, a nation that meets our conditions and renounces the use of terrorism should not face this sanction." A White House fact sheet from December 17, 2014, indicated that the Secretary of State was to provide a report to the President within six months regarding Cuba's support for international terrorism. (For additional information, see "Terrorism Issues" below.)

Increase in Travel, Commerce, and the Flow of Information to and from Cuba

The White House announced a number of policy changes to implement this third step. The changes build upon previous steps that President Obama took in 2009, when he lifted all restrictions on family travel and remittances to family members in Cuba, and in 2011, when he took action to increase purposeful travel to Cuba, such as people-to-people educational trips.

Just as in 2009 and 2011, the President's new initiative required changes to U.S. embargo regulations administered by the Department of the Treasury, Office of Foreign Assets Control (CACR; 31 CFR Part 515) and the Department of Commerce, Bureau of Industry and Security (EAR; 15 CFR Parts 730-774). Such changes fall within the scope of the President's discretionary licensing authority to make changes to the embargo regulations.

The two agencies issued amendments to the CACR and the EAR that went into effect on January 16, 2015.[68] The regulations included changes in the following areas:

- **Travel and Remittances.** The amended Treasury regulations authorize a general license for the existing 12 categories of authorized travel in the CACR, meaning that travelers who fall under these categories do not have to apply to the Treasury Department for permission. Authorized travelers will also be permitted to use U.S. credit and debit cards once U.S. financial institutions offer these services. The regulations also increase the amount of permissible remittances by U.S. persons to Cuban nationals, and unlimited remittances will be permitted for certain activities related to humanitarian projects, the promotion of civil society, and the development of private businesses. (For more details, see "Restrictions on Travel and Remittances" below.)

- **Trade and Telecommunications.** The Commerce regulations expand commercial exports to Cuba of certain goods and services to empower Cuba's nascent private sector, including authorization for certain building materials for private residential construction, goods for use by private sector Cuban entrepreneurs, and agricultural equipment for small farmers. The Treasury regulations also revise the definition of "payment of cash in advance" required by TSRA for authorized trade with Cuba to specify that it means "cash before transfer of title" for payment. Certain goods and services produced by independent Cuban entrepreneurs (as determined by the State Department) will be eligible to be imported into the United States.[69]
- The Commerce regulations permit the commercial export of certain consumer communication devices, related software, applications, hardware, and services, and items for the establishment and update of communications-related systems; previously such exports were limited to donations. They also permit the export of items for telecommunications, including access to the Internet, use of Internet services, infrastructure creation, and upgrades. An expanded Treasury Department general license authorizes transactions to provide commercial telecommunications services in Cuba or link third countries and Cuba. An updated general license allows for U.S. persons to make payments to a telecommunications operator located in Cuba for services provided to Cuban individuals.
- **Financial Services.** The Treasury regulations permit U.S. financial institutions to open correspondent accounts at Cuban financial institutions to facilitate the processing of authorized transactions, including payment for U.S. exports and for travel services.

When the President unveiled his policy changes, he acknowledged that he does not have the authority to lift the embargo because it was codified into law (Section 102(h) of the LIBERTAD Act). However, the President maintained that he looks forward to engaging Congress in a debate about lifting the embargo. As noted above, the LIBERTAD Act ties the lifting of the embargo to conditions in Cuba (including that a democratically elected government is in place). Lifting the overall economic embargo at this time would require amending or repealing the LIBERTAD Act as well as other statutes that have provisions impeding normal economic relations with Cuba, such as the

Foreign Assistance Act of 1961, the Cuban Democracy Act of 1992, and the Trade Sanctions Reform and Export Enhancement Act of 2000.

The President also indicated that his Administration was prepared to have Cuba participate in the Summit of the Americas to be held in Panama from April 10 to 11, 2015. The White House emphasized that human rights and democracy will be key themes of the summit and asserted that Cuban civil society must be allowed to participate with civil society from other countries. Cuba's potential participation in the summit had been a policy challenge for the Administration since it had opposed Cuba's participation in the 2012 Summit of the Americas in Colombia. Several Latin American nations had vowed not to participate in the 2015 summit if Cuba was not invited.

Debate on the Direction of U.S. Policy

Over the years, although U.S. policymakers have agreed on the overall objectives of U.S. policy toward Cuba—to help bring democracy and respect for human rights to the island—there have been several schools of thought about how to achieve those objectives. Some have advocated a policy of keeping maximum pressure on the Cuban government until reforms are enacted, while continuing efforts to support the Cuban people. Others argue for an approach, sometimes referred to as constructive engagement, that would lift some U.S. sanctions that they believe are hurting the Cuban people and move toward engaging Cuba in dialogue. Still others call for a swift normalization of U.S.-Cuban relations by lifting the U.S. embargo. Legislative initiatives introduced over the past decade have reflected these three policy approaches.

Dating back to 2000, there have been efforts in Congress to ease U.S. sanctions, with one or both houses at times approving amendments to appropriations measures that would have eased U.S. sanctions on Cuba. Until 2009, these provisions were stripped out of final enacted measures, in part because of presidential veto threats. In 2009, Congress took action to ease some restrictions on travel to Cuba, marking the first time that Congress has eased Cuba sanctions since the approval of the Trade Sanctions Reform and Export Enhancement Act of 2000. In light of Fidel Castro's departure as head of government and the gradual economic changes being made by Raúl Castro, some observers had called for a reexamination of U.S. policy toward Cuba. In this new context, two broad policy approaches were advanced to contend with change in Cuba: an approach that called for maintaining the U.S. dual-track policy of isolating the Cuban government while providing support to the Cuban people and an approach aimed at influencing the attitudes of the Cuban government and Cuban society through increased contact and engagement.

The Obama Administration's December 2014 change of U.S. policy from one of isolation to one of engagement and moving toward the normalization of relations has highlighted divisions in Congress over Cuba policy. Some Members of Congress lauded the Administration's actions as in the best interests of the United States and a better way to support change in Cuba, while other Members strongly criticized the President for not obtaining concessions from Cuba to advance human rights. Some Members have vowed to oppose the Administration's efforts toward normalization, while others have, as in the past, introduced legislation to normalize relations with Cuba by lifting the embargo in its entirety or in part easing some aspects of it.

In general, those who advocate easing U.S. sanctions on Cuba make several policy arguments. They assert that if the United States moderated its policy toward Cuba—through increased travel, trade, and dialogue—then the seeds of reform would be planted, which would stimulate forces for peaceful change on the island. They stress the importance to the United States of avoiding violent change in Cuba, with the prospect of a mass exodus to the United States. They argue that since the demise of Cuba's communist government does not appear imminent, even without Fidel Castro at the helm, the United States should espouse a more pragmatic approach in trying to bring about change in Cuba. Supporters of changing policy also point to broad international support for lifting the U.S. embargo, to the missed opportunities for U.S. businesses because of the unilateral nature of the embargo, and to the increased suffering of the Cuban people because of the embargo. Proponents of change also argue that the United States should be consistent in its policies with the world's few remaining communist governments, including China and Vietnam.

On the other side, opponents of lifting U.S. sanctions maintain that the two-track policy of isolating Cuba, but reaching out to the Cuban people through measures of support, is the best means for realizing political change in Cuba. They point out that the Cuban Liberty and Democratic Solidarity Act of 1996 sets forth the steps that Cuba needs to take in order for the United States to normalize relations. They argue that softening U.S. policy without concrete Cuban reforms would boost the Castro government, politically and economically, and facilitate the survival of the communist regime. Opponents of softening U.S. policy argue that the United States should stay the course in its commitment to democracy and human rights in Cuba and that sustained sanctions can work. Opponents of loosening U.S. sanctions further argue that Cuba's failed economic policies, not the U.S. embargo, are the causes of Cuba's difficult living conditions.

Public opinion polls show a majority of Americans support normalizing relations with Cuba, although the number is more closely split among Cuban Americans in Miami-Dade County in Florida. A February 2014 poll by the Atlantic Council found that 56% of respondents nationwide supported normalizing or engaging more directly in Cuba and that 63% of respondents in Florida supported such a change.[70] Since the early 1990s, Florida International University (FIU) has conducted polling in the Cuban-American community in Miami-Dade County regarding U.S. policy toward Cuba. FIU's 2014 poll, issued in June 2014, showed a slight majority of Cuban Americans in Miami-Dade County, 52%, opposed the embargo, although that dropped to 51% among registered voters. The FIU poll also showed that a large majority of Cuban Americans in Miami Dade, 69%, supported the lifting of travel restrictions for all Americans to travel to Cuba.[71]

In the aftermath of President Obama's announcement in December 2014 to reestablish diplomatic relations and move toward normalization, opinion polls showed strong support. For example, an NBC News/*Wall Street Journal* poll from January 2015 showed 60% approval for reestablishing diplomatic relations, and a Pew Research Center poll from January 2015 showed 63% in favor of reestablishing diplomatic relations and 66% in favor ending the embargo on Cuba.[72] A survey of Cuban Americans conducted in December 2014 showed that 48% opposed the decision to begin normalizing relations with Cuba, while 44% supported it.[73]

SELECTED ISSUES IN U.S.-CUBAN RELATIONS

For many years, Congress has played an active role in U.S. policy toward Cuba through the enactment of legislative initiatives and oversight on the numerous issues that comprise policy toward Cuba. These include U.S. economic sanctions on Cuba, such as restrictions on travel, remittances, and agricultural and medical exports; human rights issues, including funding and oversight of U.S.-government sponsored democracy and human rights projects; funding and oversight for U.S.-government sponsored broadcasting to Cuba (Radio and TV Martí); terrorism issues, including Cuba's designation as a state sponsor of international terrorism; migration issues; bilateral anti-drug cooperation; and U.S. claims for property confiscated by the Cuban government.

Restrictions on Travel and Remittances

Restrictions on travel to Cuba have been a key and often contentious component of U.S. efforts to isolate the communist government of Fidel Castro for much of the past 50+ years. Over time there have been numerous changes to the restrictions and for five years, from 1977 until 1982, there were no restrictions on travel. Restrictions on travel and remittances to Cuba are part of the CACR, the overall embargo regulations administered by the Treasury Department's Office of Foreign Assets Control. Under the George W. Bush Administration, enforcement of U.S. restrictions on Cuba travel increased, and restrictions on travel and on private remittances to Cuba were tightened.

Under the Obama Administration, Congress took legislative action in March 2009 easing restrictions on family travel and on travel related to U.S. agricultural and medical sales to Cuba (P.L. 111-8, Sections 620 and 621 of Division D). In April 2009, the Obama Administration went further when the President announced that he was lifting *all* restrictions on family travel as well as restrictions on cash remittances to family members in Cuba. In January 2011, the Obama Administration made a series of changes further easing restrictions on travel and remittances to Cuba. The measures (1) increased purposeful travel to Cuba related to religious, educational, and journalistic activities, including people-to-people travel exchanges; (2) allowed any U.S. person to send remittances to non-family members in Cuba (up to $500 per quarter) and made it easier for religious institutions to send remittances for religious activities; and (3) allowed U.S. international airports to become eligible to provide services to licensed charter flights to and from Cuba. In most respects, these new measures were similar to policies that were undertaken by the Clinton Administration in 1999 but subsequently curtailed by the Bush Administration in 2003 and 2004.

As noted above, just after the adjournment of the 113th Congress, President Obama announced major changes in U.S. policy toward Cuba on December 17, 2014. These changes included the provision for general licenses for the 12 existing categories of travel to Cuba: (1) family visits; (2) official business of the U.S. government, foreign governments, and certain intergovernmental organizations; (3) journalistic activity; (4) professional research and professional meetings; (5) educational activities; (6) religious activities; (7) public performances, clinics, workshops, athletic and other competitions, and exhibitions; (8) support for the Cuban people; (9) humanitarian projects (now including microfinancing projects); (10) activities of private foundations or research or educational institutes; (11) exportation, importation, or transmission of information or information materials; and (12) certain export transactions that may be considered for authorization under existing regulations and guidelines.

Before the policy change, travelers under several of these categories had to apply for a specific license from the Treasury Department before traveling. Under the new regulations, both travel agents and airlines are able to provide services for travel to Cuba without the need to obtain a specific license. U.S. credit and debit cards will also be permitted for use by authorized travelers to Cuba, and two major U.S. credit card companies have already announced that such services would begin soon. Authorized travelers will no longer have a per diem limit for expenditures, as in the past, and can bring back up to $400 worth of goods from Cuba, with no more than $100 worth of tobacco products and alcohol combined.

Despite the easing of travel restrictions, travel to Cuba solely for tourist activities remains prohibited. Section 910(b) of TSRA prohibits travel-related transaction for tourist activities, which are defined as any activity not expressly authorized in the 12 categories of travel in the CACR (31 CFR 515.560).

The Obama Administration's change in policy also increased the amount of remittances that can be sent by any U.S. person to non-family members in Cuba to $2,000 per quarter (up from the previous limit of $500 per quarter). Authorized travelers will also be permitted to carry up to $10,000 in remittances to Cuba, up from the previous limit of $3,000. Remittances to individuals and independent nongovernmental organizations (NGOs) in Cuba are authorized without limit for humanitarian projects; activities of recognized human rights organizations, independent organizations designed to promote a rapid peaceful transition to democracy, and of individuals and NGOs that promote independent activity to strengthen civil society; and the development of private businesses, including small farms.

Major arguments made for lifting the Cuba travel ban altogether are that it abridges the rights of ordinary Americans to travel; it hinders efforts to influence conditions in Cuba and may be aiding Castro by helping restrict the flow of information; and Americans can travel to other countries with communist or authoritarian governments. Major arguments in opposition to lifting the Cuba travel ban are that more American travel would support Castro's rule by providing his government with potentially millions of dollars in hard currency; that there are legal provisions allowing travel to Cuba for humanitarian purposes that are used by thousands of Americans each year; and that the President should be free to restrict travel for foreign policy reasons. With regard to remittances, supporters of the Obama Administration's recent action argue that it can help support civil society and the country's nascent private sector. Those opposed contend that the Cuban regime benefits from increased remittances by the money it accrues from taxes on private sector activity as well as fees for the exchange of U.S. dollars.

Legislative Activity

Several legislative initiatives introduced in the 114th Congress would lift remaining restrictions on travel and remittances. Two bills would lift the overall embargo, H.R. 274 (Rush) and H.R. 403 (Rangel), including restrictions on travel and remittances. One bill, H.R. 635 (Rangel), would facilitate the export of U.S. agricultural and medical exports to Cuba and also lift travel restrictions. Three bills would focus solely on prohibiting restrictions on travel to Cuba: H.R. 634 (Rangel), H.R. 664 (Sanford), and S. 299 (Flake).

U.S. Exports and Sanctions[74]

U.S. commercial medical exports to Cuba have been authorized since the early 1990s pursuant to the Cuban Democracy Act of 1992 or CDA (P.L. 102-484, Title XVII), and commercial agricultural exports have been authorized since 2001 pursuant to the Trade Sanctions Reform and Export Enhancement Act of 2000 or TSRA (P.L. 106-387, Title IX), but with numerous restrictions and licensing requirements. The CDA has an onsite verification requirement for medical exports to Cuba that the exported item is to be used for which it was intended and only for the use and benefit of the Cuban people. TSRA allows for one-year export licenses for selling agricultural commodities to Cuba, although no U.S. government assistance, foreign assistance, export assistance, credits, or credit guarantees are available to finance such exports. TSRA also denies exporters access to U.S. private commercial financing or credit; all transactions must be conducted in cash in advance or with financing from third countries.

Cuba purchased over $5 billion in U.S. products from 2001-2014, largely agricultural products, and for most years since 2002, the United States has been Cuba's largest supplier of agricultural products. U.S. exports to Cuba rose from about $7 million in 2001 to $404 million in 2004 and to a high of $712 million in 2008, far higher than in previous years, in part because of the rise in food prices and because of Cuba's increased food needs in the aftermath of several hurricanes and tropical storms that severely damaged the country's agricultural sector. U.S. exports to Cuba declined considerably from 2009 through 2011, amounting to $363 million in 2010 and 2011, while in 2012, they rose to $464 million, a 28% increase (see **Figure 3**).[75] Part of the increase in 2012 can be attributed to an increase in Cuba's import needs because of damage to the agricultural sector in eastern Cuba caused by Hurricane Sandy in October. U.S. exports to Cuba resumed falling in 2013 and 2014, to $359 million and $299 million, respectively. Looking at the composition of U.S. exports to Cuba from 2012-2014, the leading products have been poultry, corn, soybean oilcake, and soybeans, although corn exports declined considerably in this period.

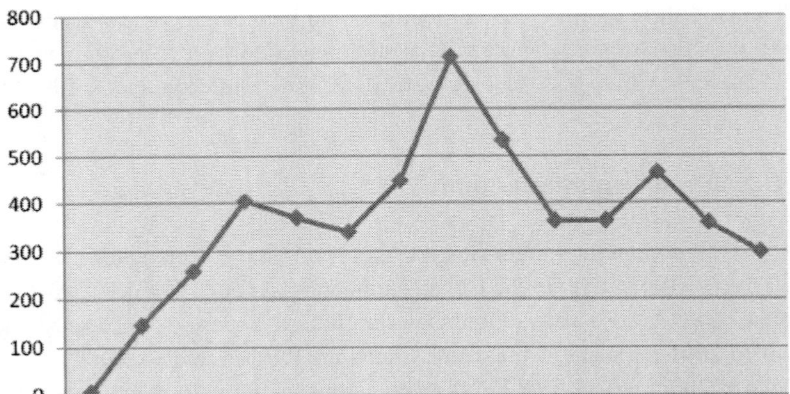

	2001	2002	2003	2004	2005	2006	2007	2008	2009	2010	2011	2012	2013	2014
U.S. $ mil.	7	146	259	404	369	340	447	712	533	363	363	464	359	299

Source: Created by CRS using information from the Global Trade Atlas, which uses data from the Department of Commerce.

Figure 3. U.S. Exports to Cuba, 2001-2014; (U.S. $ millions).

President Obama's policy changes in Cuba unveiled in December 2014 included several measures that could potentially expand commercial exports to Cuba.

- U.S. institutions will be permitted to open correspondent accounts at Cuban financial institutions to facilitate the processing of authorized transactions.
- The definition of the term "cash in advance" for payment for U.S. exports to Cuba will be revised to specify that it means "cash before transfer of title." In 2005, the Treasury Department's Office of Foreign Assets Control had clarified that "payment of cash in advance" meant that the payment for the goods had to be received prior to the shipment of the goods from the port at which they were loaded in the United States. For FY2010 and FY2011, Congress had temporarily overturned OFAC's clarification of the term in omnibus appropriations legislation (Division C, Section 619 of P.L. 111-117, and continued by reference in Division B, Section 1101 of P.L. 112-10). The recent change means that payment can once again occur before an export shipment is offloaded in Cuba, rather than before the shipment leaves a U.S. port.
- Commercial exports to Cuba of certain goods and services to empower Cuba's nascent private sector are authorized, including for certain building materials for private residential construction, goods for use by private sector Cuban entrepreneurs, and agricultural equipment for small farmers.
- The commercial export of certain consumer communication devices, related software, applications, hardware, and services, and items for the establishment and update of communications-related systems is authorized; previously such exports were limited to donations. The export of items for telecommunications, including access to the Internet, use of Internet services, infrastructure creation, and upgrades, is also authorized.

Among the reasons for the overall decline in U.S. exports to Cuba in recent years, analysts cite Cuba's shortage of hard currency; credits and other arrangements offered by other governments to purchase their countries' products; and Cuba's perception that its efforts to motivate U.S. companies, organizations, local and state officials, and Members of Congress to push for change in U.S. sanctions policy toward Cuba have been ineffective.[76] Some agricultural experts are skeptical as to whether the Obama Administration's recent changes in policy will lead to a significant increase in U.S. agricultural exports to Cuba, pointing out that other countries will still be able to offer better terms to Cuba than the United States because of restrictions on financing and credit.[77]

The U.S. International Trade Commission (USITC) produced a study in 2007 analyzing the effects of both U.S. government financing restrictions for agricultural exports to Cuba and U.S. travel restrictions on the level of U.S. agricultural sales to Cuba.[78] At the time of the study, the U.S. share of various Cuban agricultural imports was estimated to range from 0% to 99% depending on the commodity. If U.S. financing restrictions were lifted, the study estimated that the U.S. share of Cuban agricultural, fish, and forest products imports would rise to between one-half and two-thirds. According to the study, if travel restrictions for all U.S. citizens were lifted, the influx of U.S. tourists would be significant in the short term and would boost demand for imported agricultural products, particularly high-end products for the tourist sector. If both financing and travel restrictions were lifted, the study found that the largest gains in U.S. exports to Cuba would be for fresh fruits and vegetables, milk powder, processed foods, wheat, and dry beans.

In 2009, the USITC issued a working paper that updated the agency's 2007 study on U.S. agricultural sales to Cuba. The update concluded that if U.S. restrictions on financing and travel had been lifted in 2008, U.S. agricultural exports to Cuba would have increased between $216 million and $478 million, and the U.S. share of Cuba's agricultural imports would have increased from 38% to between 49% and 64%.[79] Among the U.S. agricultural products that would have benefited the most were wheat, rice, beef, pork, processed foods, and fish products.

In response to a request by the Senate Finance Committee in December 2014, the USITC began another investigation, expected to be completed in September 2015, examining the effects of restrictions on trade and travel to Cuba on the export of U.S. goods and services, including digitally traded goods and services. The report is to include an estimate of the export of such U.S. goods and services to Cuba in the event that U.S. restrictions are lifted.[80]

Legislative Activity

Several legislative initiatives introduced in the 114th Congress would lift restrictions on exports to Cuba. Two bills would lift the overall embargo, H.R. 274 (Rush) and H.R. 403 (Rangel), including restriction on exports to Cuba in the CDA and TSRA. One bill, H.R. 635 (Rangel), among its various provisions, has the goal of facilitating the export of U.S. agricultural and medical exports to Cuba by permanently redefining the term "payment of cash in advance" to mean that payment is received before the transfer of title and release and control of the commodity to the purchaser; authorizing direct transfers between Cuban and U.S. financial institutions for products exported under the terms of TSRA; establishing an export promotion program for U.S. agricultural exports to Cuba; prohibiting restriction on travel to Cuba; and repealing the onsite verification requirement for medical exports to Cuba under the CDA. In the Senate, S. 491 (Klobuchar), would remove many provisions of law restricting trade and other relations with Cuba, including certain restrictions in the CDA and TSRA.

Trademark Sanction[81]

For some 15 years, the United States has imposed a trademark sanction specifically related to Cuba. A provision in the FY1999 omnibus appropriations measure (§211 of Division A, Title II, P.L. 105-277, signed into law October 21, 1998) prevents the United States from accepting payment for trademark registrations and renewals from Cuban nationals that were used in connection with a business or assets in Cuba that were confiscated, unless the original owner of the trademark has consented. The provision prohibits U.S. courts from recognizing such trademarks without the consent of the original owner. The measure was enacted because of a dispute between the French spirits company, Pernod Ricard, and the Bermuda-based Bacardi Ltd. Pernod Ricard entered into a joint venture in 1993 with the Cuban government to produce and export Havana Club rum. Bacardi maintains that it holds the right to the Havana Club name because in 1995 it entered into an agreement for the Havana Club trademark with the Arechabala family, who had originally produced the rum until its assets and property were confiscated by the Cuban government in 1960. Although Pernod Ricard cannot market Havana Club in the United States because of the trade embargo, it wants to protect its future distribution rights should the embargo be lifted.

The European Union initiated World Trade Organization (WTO) dispute settlement proceedings in June 2000, maintaining that the U.S. law violates the Agreement on Trade-Related Aspects of Intellectual Property (TRIPS). In January 2002, the WTO ultimately found that the trademark sanction violated WTO provisions on national treatment and most-favored-nation obligations in the TRIPS Agreement.[82] On March 28, 2002, the United States agreed that it would come into compliance with the WTO ruling through legislative action by January 3, 2003.[83] That deadline was extended several times since no legislative action had been taken to bring Section 211 into compliance with the

WTO ruling. On July 1, 2005, however, in an EU-U.S. bilateral agreement, the EU agreed that it would not request authorization to retaliate at that time, but reserved the right to do so at a future date, and the United States agreed not to block a future EU request.[84] In June 2013, EU officials reportedly raised the issue of U.S. compliance at a WTO Dispute Settlement Body meeting, maintaining that there has been enough time for the United States to settle the issue, while U.S. officials maintained that relevant bills were before the U.S. Congress.[85]

On August 3, 2006, the U.S. Patent and Trademark Office announced that Cuba's Havana Club trademark registration was "cancelled/expired," a week after the Treasury Department's Office of Foreign Assets Control denied a Cuban government company the license that it needed to renew the registration of the trademark.[86] On March 29, 2011, the U.S. Court of Appeals of the District of Columbia upheld the decision to deny the renewal of the trademark.[87]

Legislative Activity

In Congress, two different approaches have been advocated for a number of years to bring Section 211 into compliance with the WTO ruling. Some want a narrow fix in which Section 211 would be amended so that it applies to all persons claiming rights in trademarks confiscated by Cuba, whatever their nationality, instead of being limited to designated nationals, meaning Cuban nationals. Advocates of this approach argue that it would treat all holders of U.S. trademarks equally. Others want Section 211 repealed altogether. They argue that the law endangers over 5,000 trademarks of over 500 U.S. companies registered in Cuba.[88] In the 114th Congress, several bills have been introduced that would repeal Section 211: H.R. 274 (Rush); H.R. 403 (Rangel); H.R. 635 (Rangel); and H.R. 735 (Serrano).

U.S. Funding to Support Democracy and Human Rights

Since 1996, the United States has provided assistance—through the U.S. Agency for International Development (USAID), the State Department, and the National Endowment for Democracy (NED)—to increase the flow of information on democracy, human rights, and free enterprise to Cuba.

USAID and State Department efforts are largely funded through Economic Support Funds (ESF) in the annual foreign operations appropriations bill. From FY1996 to FY2014, Congress appropriated some

$264 million in funding for Cuba democracy efforts.[89] In recent years, this included $45.3 million for FY2008 and $20 million in each fiscal year from FY2009 through FY2012, $19.3 million in FY2013, and $20 million in FY2014. The Administration's FY2015 request was for $20 million; the amount that will be provided is uncertain since no amount was specified in the FY2015 omnibus appropriations measure (P.L. 113-235).

The Administration's request for FY2016 is $20 million. According to the request, assistance will support fundamental freedoms and respect for human rights, help victims of political repression and their families, and strengthen independent Cuban civil society and freedom of expression.

Generally, as provided in appropriations measures, ESF has to be obligated within two fiscal years. In recent years, the obligation has been notified to Congress (as required in appropriations legislation) just a few months before the end of the two years (e.g., the obligation of FY2013 assistance was notified in July 2014). USAID in the past received the majority of this funding, but the State Department began receiving a portion in FY2004 and in recent years has been allocated more funding than USAID. The State Department generally has transferred a portion of the Cuba assistance that it administers to NED. For FY2014, Congress stipulated that not less than $7.5 million shall be provided directly to NED while not more than $10 million shall be administered by the State Department; Congress also stipulated that no ESF appropriated under the Act may be obligated by USAID for any new programs or activities in Cuba (P.L. 113-76).

USAID's Cuba program has supported a variety of U.S.-based nongovernmental organizations with the goals of promoting a rapid, peaceful transition to democracy, helping develop civil society, and building solidarity with Cuba's human rights activists. USAID maintains on its website that current USAID program partners are Grupo de Apoyo a la Democracia, $3 million (2012-2015); International Republican Institute, $3 million (2012-2015); New America Foundation, $4.3 million (2012-2015); and Pan-American Development Foundation, $3.9 million (2011-2015). (See USAID's Cuba program website at http://www.usaid.gov/where-we-work/ latin-american-and-caribbean/cuba.)

NED is not a U.S. government agency but an independent nongovernmental organization that receives U.S. government funding. Its Cuba program is funded by the organization's regular appropriations by Congress as well as by funding from the State Department. Until FY2008, NED's democratization assistance for Cuba had been funded largely through the annual Commerce, Justice, and State (CJS) appropriations measure, but is now funded through the State Department, Foreign Operations and Related Agencies appropriations measure. As noted above, for FY2014, Congress stipulated that not less than $7.5 million of democracy assistance for Cuba be provided directly to NED for activities and programs in Cuba. According to NED, its Cuba funding in recent years has been as follows: $1.65 million in FY2011; $2.6 million in FY2012; and $3.4 million in FY2013.

Oversight of U.S. Democracy Assistance to Cuba

The U.S. Government Accountability Office (GAO) has issued several reports since 2006 examining USAID and State Department democracy programs for Cuba. In 2006, GAO issued a report examining programs from 1996 through 2005 and concluded that the U.S. program had significant problems and needed better management and oversight. According to GAO, internal controls, for both the awarding of Cuba program grants and the oversight of grantees, "do not provide adequate assurance that the funds are being used properly and that grantees are in compliance with applicable law and regulations."[90] Investigative news reports on the program maintained that high shipping costs and lax oversight had diminished its effectiveness.[91]

GAO issued a second report in 2008 examining USAID's Cuba democracy program.[92] The report lauded the steps that USAID had taken since 2006 to address problems with its Cuba program and improve oversight of the assistance. These included awarding all grants competitively since 2006, hiring more staff for the program office since January 2008, and contracting for financial services in April 2008 to enhance oversight of grantees. The GAO report also noted that USAID had worked to strengthen program oversight through pre-award and follow-up reviews, improving grantee internal controls and implementation plans, and providing guidance and monitoring about permitted types of assistance and cost sharing. The 2008 GAO report also maintained, however, that USAID had not staffed the Cuba program to the level needed for effective grant oversight. GAO recommended that USAID (1) ensure that its Cuba program office is staffed at the level that is needed to fully implement planned monitoring activities and (2) periodically assess the Cuba program's overall efforts to address and reduce grantee risks, especially regarding internal controls, procurement practices, expenditures, and compliance with laws and regulations.

More recently, in January 2013, GAO issued its third report on Cuba democracy programs.[93] The report concluded that USAID had improved its performance and financial monitoring of implementing partners' use of program funds, but found that the State Department's financial monitoring had gaps. Both agencies were reported to be taking steps to improve financial monitoring. GAO recommended that the Secretary of State take two actions to strengthen the agency's ability to monitor the use of Cuba democracy program funds: use a risk-based approach for program audits that considers specific indicators for program partners and obtain sufficient information to approve implementing partners' use of subpartners.

In April 2014, an Associated Press investigative report alleged that USAID, as part of its democracy promotion efforts for Cuba, had established a "Cuban Twitter" known as ZunZuneo, a communications network designed as a "covert" program "to undermine" Cuba's communist government built with "secret shell companies" and financed through foreign banks. According to the press report, the project, which was used by thousands of Cubans, lasted more than two years until it ended in 2012.[94] USAID, which strongly contested the report, issued a statement and facts about the ZunZuneo program. It maintained that program was not "covert," but rather that, just as in other places where it is not always welcome, the agency maintained a "discreet profile" on the project to minimize risk to staff and partners and work safely.[95] Some Members of Congress strongly criticized USAID for not providing sufficient information to Congress about the program when funding was appropriated, while other Members strongly defended the agency and the program.

In August 2014, the Associated Press reported on another U.S.-funded democracy program for Cuba in which a USAID contractor sent about a dozen youth from several Latin American countries (Costa Rica, Peru, and Venezuela) in 2010 and 2011 to Cuba to participate in civic programs, including an HIV-prevention workshop, with the alleged goal to "identify potential social-change actors" in Cuba. The AP report alleged that "the assignment was to recruit young Cubans to anti-government activism under the guise of civic programs."[96] USAID responded in a statement maintaining that the AP report "made sensational claims against aid workers for supporting civil society programs and striving to give voice to these democratic aspirations."[97]

Radio and TV Martí

U.S.-government-sponsored radio and television broadcasting to Cuba—Radio and TV Martí— began in 1985 and 1990, respectively. According to the *Broadcasting Board of Governors (BBG) FY2015 Congressional Budget*

Request, Radio and TV Martí "inform and engage the people of Cuba by providing a reliable and credible source of news and information." The BBG's Office of Cuba Broadcasting uses "a mix of media, including shortwave, medium wave, direct-to-home satellite, Internet, flash drives, and DVDs to help reach audiences in Cuba."[98]

Until October 1999, U.S.-government-funded international broadcasting programs had been a primary function of the United States Information Agency (USIA). When USIA was abolished and its functions were merged into the Department of State at the beginning of FY2000, the BBG became an independent agency that included such entities as the Voice of America (VOA), Radio Free Europe/Radio Liberty (RFE/RL), Radio Free Asia, and the Office of Cuba Broadcasting (OCB), which manages Radio and TV Marti. OCB is headquartered in Miami, FL. Legislation in the 104th Congress (P.L. 104-134) required the relocation of OCB from Washington, DC, to South Florida. The move began in 1996 and was completed in 1998.

According to the BBG, the OCB uses multiple web domains and anti-censorship tools such as web-based proxies to reach Internet users in Cuba. Since 2011, the OCB has used SMS messaging to communicate with audiences in Cuba, allowing OCB to "push" information to mobile phone users in Cuba in a manner that is difficult to filter. The OCB's website, martinoticias.com, began streaming Radio and TV Martí programming 24 hours a day in 2013. It has also launched a YouTube Channel, Facebook page, and Twitter feed.

From FY1984 through FY2015, Congress appropriated about $797 million for broadcasting to Cuba. In recent years, funding amounted to $28 million in FY2012, $26 million in FY2013, and an estimated $27 million in FY2014. The FY2015 request was for $23 million, and Congress ultimately appropriated $27 million in the FY2015 omnibus appropriations measure (P.L. 113- 235). The explanatory statement to the measure also indicated that funds may be transferred to the OCB from appropriated ESF to restore program reductions.

Both Radio and TV Martí have at times been the focus of controversies, including questions about adherence to broadcast standards. There have been various attempts over the years to cut funding for the programs, especially for TV Martí, which has not had much of an audience because of Cuban jamming efforts. From 1990 through 2008, there were numerous government studies and audits of the OCB, including investigations by the GAO, by a 1994 congressionally established Advisory Panel on Radio and TV Martí, by the

State Department Office Inspector General (OIG), and by the combined State Department/BBG Office Inspector General.[99]

In 2009, GAO issued a report asserting that the best available research suggests that Radio and TV Martí's audience is small, and cited telephone surveys since 2003 showing that less than 2% of respondents reported tuning in to Radio or TV Martí during the past week. With regard to TV Martí viewership, according to the report, all of the IBB's telephone surveys since 2003 show that less than 1% of respondents said that they had watched TV Martí during the past week. According to the GAO report, the IBB surveys show that there was no increase in reported TV Martí viewership following the beginning of AeroMartí and DirecTV satellite broadcasting in 2006.The GAO report also cited concerns with adherence to relevant domestic laws and international standards, including the domestic dissemination of OCB programming, inappropriate advertisements during OCB programming, and TV Martí's interference with Cuban broadcasts.[100]

In 2010, the Senate Foreign Relations Committee majority issued a staff report that concluded that Radio and TV Martí "continue to fail in their efforts to influence Cuban society, politics, and policy." The report cited problems with adherence to broadcast standards, audience size, and Cuban government jamming. Among its recommendations, the report called for the IBB to move the Office of Cuba Broadcasting back to Washington, DC, and integrate it fully into the Voice of America.[101]

In 2011, GAO issued a report examining the extent to which the BBG's strategic plan for broadcasting required by the conference report to the FY2010 Consolidated Appropriations measure (H.Rept. 111-366 to H.R. 3288/P.L. 111-117) met the requirements established in the legislation. GAO found that BBG's strategic plan lacked key information and only partially addressed issues raised by Congress, including on estimated audience size and an analysis of other options for disseminating news and information to Cuba. The report stated that the BBG can develop and provide more information to Congress, including an analysis of the cost savings opportunities of sharing resources between Radio and TV Martí and the Voice of America's Latin America Division.[102]

Terrorism Issues[103]

As noted above, in December 2014, President Obama called for the Secretary of State to review Cuba's designation as a state sponsor of terrorism, with a report due to the President within six months. Critics of retaining Cuba on the terrorism list maintain that it is a holdover from the Cold War. They argue that domestic political considerations keep Cuba on the terrorism list and maintain that Cuba's presence on the list diverts U.S. attention from struggles against serious terrorist threats. Those who support keeping Cuba on the terrorism list argue that there is ample evidence that Cuba supports terrorism. They point to the government's continued hosting of members of foreign terrorist organizations and U.S. fugitives from justice and Cuba's involvement in a weapons transfer to North Korea in contravention of U.N. sanctions (see "Cuba's Foreign Relations" above).

Cuba was added to the State Department's list of states sponsoring international terrorism in 1982 pursuant to Section 6(j) of the EAA and other laws because of its alleged ties to international terrorism and support for terrorist groups in Latin America, and it has remained on the list since that time. Under the EAA and other provisions of law, certain trade benefits, most foreign aid, support in the international financial institutions, and other benefits are restricted or denied to countries named as state sponsors of international terrorism.

As set forth in Section 6(j) of the EAA, a country's retention on the state sponsors of terrorism list may be rescinded by the President in two ways. The first option is for the President to submit a report to Congress certifying that there has been a fundamental change in the leadership and policies of the government and that the government is not supporting acts of international terrorism and is providing assurances that it will not support such acts in the future. The second option is for the President to submit a report to Congress, at least 45 days in advance, justifying the rescission and certifying that the government has not provided any support for international terrorism during the preceding six months, and has provided assurances that it will not support such acts in the future. If the President makes the decision to remove Cuba from the list, the State Department has indicated that the second option would utilized, with the President submitting a report to Congress 45 days before the rescission would take effect.

In addition to Section 6(j) of the EAA, there are two other provisions of law that authorize the designation of a foreign government as a state sponsor of acts of international terrorism: Section 620A of the Foreign Assistance Act (FAA) of 1961 (22 U.S.C. 2371) and Section 40 of the Arms Export Control Act (AECA) (22 U.S.C. 2780).[104] Of the three statutes, only the AECA has an explicit provision allowing Congress to block, via the enactment of a joint resolution, a removal of a country on the list.

Cuba had a long history of supporting revolutionary movements and governments in Latin America and Africa, but in 1992, Fidel Castro said that his country's support for insurgents abroad was a thing of the past. Cuba's change in policy was in large part due to the breakup of the Soviet Union, which resulted in the loss of billions of dollars in annual subsidies to Cuba and led to substantial Cuban economic decline.

In its *Country Reports on Terrorism 2013* report (issued April 30, 2014), the State Department stated that Cuba has long provided safe haven to members of the Basque Fatherland and Liberty (ETA) and the Revolutionary Armed Forces of Colombia (FARC). The report noted, however, that Cuba's ties to ETA have become more distant and that about eight of the two dozen ETA members in Cuba were relocated with the cooperation of the Spanish government. With regard to the FARC, the terrorism report noted that the Cuban government had been supporting and hosting peace negotiations between the FARC and the Colombian government since 2012. As in its 2011 and 2012 reports, the State Department stated in the 2013 terrorism report that "there was no indication that the Cuban government provided weapons or paramilitary training to terrorist groups."[105]

Another issue noted in the 2013 terrorism report that has been mentioned for many years in the annual report is Cuba's harboring of fugitives wanted in the United States. The report maintained that Cuba provided such support as housing, food ration books, and medical care for these individuals. U.S. fugitives from justice in Cuba include convicted murderers and numerous hijackers, most of whom entered Cuba in the 1970s and early 1980s.[106] For example, Joanne Chesimard, also known as Assata Shakur, was added to the FBI's Most Wanted Terrorist list on May 2, 2013. Chesimard was part of militant group known as the Black Liberation Army. In 1977, she was convicted for the 1973 murder of a New Jersey State Police officer and sentenced to life in prison. Chesimard escaped from prison in 1979 and, according to the FBI, lived underground before fleeing to Cuba in 1984.[107] In addition to Chesimard and other fugitives from the past, a number of U.S. fugitives from justice wanted for Medicare and other types of insurance fraud reportedly have fled to Cuba in recent years.[108] On November 6, 2013, William Potts, an American citizen who had hijacked an airplane from New Jersey to Havana in 1984, returned to the United States to face air-piracy charges; he had served 14 years in a Cuban jail for his crime.[109]

While the United States and Cuba have an extradition treaty in place dating to 1905, in practice the treaty has not been utilized. Instead, for more than a decade, Cuba has returned wanted fugitives to the United States on a case-by-case basis. For example, in 2011, U.S. Marshals picked up a husband and wife in Cuba who were wanted for a 2010 murder in New Jersey,[110] while in April 2013, Cuba returned a Florida couple who had allegedly kidnapped their own children (who had been in the custody of the mother's parents) and fled to Havana.[111] However, Cuba has generally refused to render to U.S. justice any fugitive judged by Cuba to be "political," such as Chesimard, who they believe could not receive a fair trial in the United States. Moreover, Cuba in the past has responded to U.S. extradition requests by stating that approval would be contingent upon the United States returning wanted Cuban criminals from the United States. These include the return of Luis Posada Carriles, whom Cuba accused of plotting the 1976 bombing of a Cuban jet that killed 73 people.[112]

Legislative Activity

In the 114th Congress, H.R. 274 (Rush) has a provision that would immediately rescind any determination of the Secretary of State that Cuba has repeatedly provided support for acts of international terrorism. The bill references all three statutes authorizing the designation of a country as a sponsor of acts of international terrorism: Section 6(j) of the EAA, Section 620A of the FAA, and Section 40 of the AECA.

Migration Issues[113]

Cuba and the United States reached two migration accords in 1994 and 1995 designed to stem the mass exodus of Cubans attempting to reach the United States by boat. On the minds of U.S. policymakers was the 1980 Mariel boatlift, in which 125,000 Cubans fled to the United States with the approval of Cuban officials. In response to Fidel Castro's threat to unleash another Mariel, U.S. officials reiterated U.S. resolve not to allow another exodus. Amid escalating numbers of fleeing Cubans, on August 19, 1994, President Clinton abruptly changed U.S. migration policy, under which Cubans attempting to flee their homeland were allowed into the United States, and announced that the U.S. Coast Guard and Navy would take Cubans rescued at sea to the U.S. naval base at Guantanamo Bay, Cuba. Despite the change in policy, Cubans continued fleeing in large numbers.

As a result, in early September 1994, Cuba and the United States began talks that culminated in a September 9, 1994, bilateral agreement to stem the flow of Cubans fleeing to the United States by boat. In the agreement, the

United States and Cuba agreed to facilitate safe, legal, and orderly Cuban migration to the United States, consistent with a 1984 migration agreement. The United States agreed to ensure that total legal Cuban migration to the United States would be a minimum of 20,000 each year, not including immediate relatives of U.S. citizens.

In May 1995, the United States reached another accord with Cuba under which the United States would parole the more than 30,000 Cubans housed at Guantanamo into the United States, but would intercept future Cuban migrants attempting to enter the United States by sea and would return them to Cuba. The two countries would cooperate jointly in the effort. Both countries also pledged to ensure that no action would be taken against those migrants returned to Cuba as a consequence of their attempt to immigrate illegally. On January 31, 1996, the Department of Defense announced that the last of some 32,000 Cubans intercepted at sea and housed at Guantanamo had left the U.S. Naval Station, most having been paroled into the United States.

Since the 1995 migration accord, the U.S. Coast Guard has interdicted thousands of Cubans at sea and returned them to their country. Those Cubans who reach shore are allowed to apply for permanent resident status in one year, pursuant to the Cuban Adjustment Act of 1966 (CAA, P.L. 89-732). In short, most interdictions, even in U.S. coastal waters, result in a return to Cuba, while those Cubans who touch shore are allowed to stay in the United States. This so-called "wet foot/dry foot" policy has been criticized by some as encouraging Cubans to risk their lives in order to make it to the United States and as encouraging alien smuggling. Others maintain that U.S. policy should welcome those migrants fleeing communist Cuba whether or not they are able to make it to land.

The number of Cubans interdicted at sea by the U.S. Coast Guard rose from 666 in FY2002 to a high of 2,868 in FY2007. In the three subsequent years, maritime interdictions declined significantly to 422 by FY2010 (see **Figure 4**). Major reasons for the decline were reported to include the U.S. economic downturn, more efficient coastal patrolling, and more aggressive prosecution of migrant smugglers by both the United States and Cuba.[114]

From FY2011 to FY2014, however, the number of Cubans interdicted by the Coast Guard increased each year, from 985 in FY2011 to 2,059 in FY2014. Migrant interdictions at sea in FY2015 have continued to increase, with 712 interdicted in the first quarter of the fiscal year (October-December 2014), according to the U.S. Coast Guard.[115] Speculation on the reasons for the increase in interdictions in recent years include Cuba's poor economic and political situation; the Coast Guard's more efficient methods of interdiction;

and the easing of the economic situation in the United States, making it easier for the payment of fees to migrant smugglers.[116] The U.S. State Department reports that timely and clear communication between the U.S. Coast Guard and the Cuban Border Guard (TGF) also has been a factor in increasing the rate of migrant interdiction, with the TGF providing more operationally relevant information than in the past.[117]

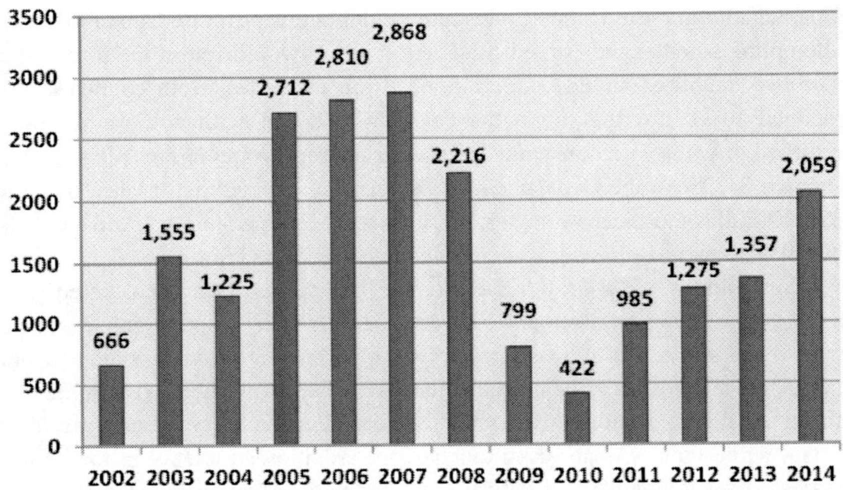

Source: Created by CRS using information provided by the United States Coast Guard, Alien Migrant Interdiction, "Total Interdictions—Fiscal Year 1982 to Present," as of December 31, 2014, current statistics available at http://www.uscg.mil/hq/cg5/cg531/AMIO/FlowStats/FY.asp.

Figure 4. Maritime Interdictions of Cubans by the U.S. Coast Guard, FY2002-FY2014.

Despite the U.S. Coast Guard's maritime interdiction program, thousands of unauthorized Cubans reach the United States each year, either by boat or, especially, at land ports of entry. According to the State Department, Cubans continue to favor land-based entry at U.S. ports of entry, especially from Mexico, but also flying directly to the United States from third countries. In FY2014, according to the State Department, a total of 24,289 Cubans presented themselves at land ports of entry, with the majority, 72%, presenting themselves at the southwest border.[118] Some press reports indicate that the number of Cuban migrants flowing to the United States increased further in the last three months of calendar year 2014, and especially since the Obama Administration announced that diplomatic relations would be restored.[119]

Semi-annual bilateral talks are held on the implementation of the 1994/1995 migration accords, alternating between Havana and Washington, DC. The most recent talks occurred on January 21, 2015, in Havana, a day before talks were held on the process of restoring diplomatic relations. The head of the U.S. delegation, Alex Lee, Deputy Assistant Secretary of State for Western Hemisphere Affairs, maintained that both countries restated their commitment under the migration accords to ensure that migration remains safe, legal, and orderly. He noted that the talks also included an exchange of ideas on other aspects of safe migration, such as the return of Cuban excludable aliens, the Cuban Family Reunification Parole Program, and the monitoring of repatriated Cuban nationals.[120] The head of the Cuban delegation, Josefina Vidal, director of the North American division of Cuba's Ministry of Foreign Relations, noted increasing cooperation and communication between both countries to confront illegal migration, alien smuggling, and immigration fraud. She also reiterated Cuba's position that the U.S. "wet foot/dry foot policy" and the CAA continue to encourage illegal immigration and alien smuggling and expressed opposition to the U.S. policy of trying to attract Cuban medical professionals in third countries to "abandon their missions."[121] U.S. officials have stated that there would be no changes to current immigration policy toward Cuba.[122]

In January 2013, the Cuban government changed its long-standing policy of requiring an exit permit and a letter of invitation from abroad for Cubans to travel abroad. Cubans are now able to travel abroad with just an updated passport and a visa issued by the country of destination, if required. Under the change in policy, Cubans can travel abroad for up to two years without forgoing their rights as Cuban citizens. The practice of requiring an exit permit had been extremely unpopular in Cuba, and the government had been considering doing away with the practice for some time. According to the Department of State, the Cuban government still requires some individuals, such as high-level government officials, doctors, lawyers, and technicians, to obtain permission to travel.[123] In addition, some dissidents out on parole or facing court action reportedly have not been permitted to travel aboard, although many prominent dissidents have traveled abroad and returned to Cuba.

Effective August 1, 2013, the State Department made nonimmigrant B-2 visas issued to Cubans for family visits, tourism, medical treatment, or other personal travel valid for five years with multiple entries. Previously these visas had been restricted to single entry for six months, and an extensive visa interview backlog had developed at the U.S. Interests Section in Havana. State

Department officials maintain that the change increases people-to-people ties and removes procedural and financial burdens on Cuban travelers.[124]

In light of Cuba's new travel policy initiated in 2013 making it easier for Cubans to travel aboard and the Administration's efforts to normalize relations with Cuba, some analysts have raised questions as to whether the United States should review its policy toward Cuban migrants as set forth in the CAA.[125] Some argue that the normalization of relations will make a special immigration policy for Cubans difficult to sustain.[126] Some critics of current policy also argue that the law is being abused by some recent Cuban arrivals who travel back and forth between Cuba and the United States regularly.[127]

Anti-Drug Cooperation

Cuba is not a major producer or consumer of illicit drugs, but its extensive shoreline and geographic location make it susceptible to narcotics smuggling operations. Drugs that enter the Cuban market are largely the result of onshore wash-ups from smuggling by high-speed boats moving drugs from Jamaica to the Bahamas, Haiti, and the United States or by small aircraft from clandestine airfields in Jamaica. For a number of years, Cuban officials have expressed concerns over the use of their waters and airspace for drug transit and about increased domestic drug use. The Cuban government has taken a number of measures to deal with the drug problem, including legislation to stiffen penalties for traffickers, increased training for counternarcotics personnel, and cooperation with a number of countries on anti-drug efforts. According to the State Department's 2014 *International Narcotics Control Strategy Report (INCSR)*, issued February 28, 2014, Cuba has a number of anti-drug-related agreements in place with other countries, including 35 bilateral agreements for counterdrug cooperation and 27 policing cooperation agreements. Since 1999, Cuba's Operation Hatchet has focused on maritime and air interdiction and the recovery of narcotics washed up on Cuban shores. As reported in the *INCSR*, Cuba reported interdicting 3 metric tons of illegal narcotics in 2012, with the overwhelming majority consisting of wash ups. Since 2003, Cuba has aggressively pursued an internal enforcement and investigation program against its incipient drug market with an effective nationwide drug prevention and awareness campaign.

Over the years, there have been varying levels of U.S.-Cuban cooperation on anti-drug efforts. In 1996, Cuban authorities cooperated with the United States in the seizure of 6.6 tons of cocaine aboard the Miami-bound *Limerick*, a Honduran-flag ship. Cuba turned over the cocaine to the United States and cooperated fully in the investigation and subsequent prosecution of two defendants in the case in the United States. Cooperation has increased since 1999, when U.S. and Cuban officials met in Havana to discuss ways of improving anti-drug cooperation. Cuba accepted an upgrading of the communications link between the Cuban Border Guard and the U.S. Coast Guard as well as the stationing of a U.S. Coast Guard Drug Interdiction Specialist (DIS) at the U.S. Interests Section in Havana. The Coast Guard official was posted to the U.S. Interests Section in September 2000, and since that time, coordination has increased.

According to the 2014 *INCSR*, the Coast Guard shares tactical information related to narcotics trafficking on a case-by-case basis and responds to Cuban information on vessels transiting through Cuban territorial seas suspected of smuggling. The report maintained that law enforcement communication gradually increased in frequency and transparency in 2013, especially concerning efforts to target drug trafficking at sea. The United States and Cuba held a "professional exchange between experts" on maritime drug interdiction that included tours of facilities, unit capabilities, and possible future joint coordination.

Cuba maintains that it wants to cooperate with the United States to combat drug trafficking and, on various occasions, has called for a bilateral anti-drug cooperation agreement with the United States.[128] In the 2011 *INCSR* (issued in March 2011) the State Department acknowledged that Cuba had presented the U.S. government with a draft bilateral accord for counternarcotics cooperation that is still under review. According to the State Department in the *INCSR*, "Structured appropriately, such an accord could advance the counternarcotics efforts undertaken by both countries." The report maintained that greater cooperation among the United States, Cuba, and its international partners—especially in the area of real-time tactical information-sharing and improved tactics, techniques, and procedures—would likely lead to increased interdictions and disruptions of illegal trafficking. These positive U.S. statements regarding a potential bilateral anti-drug cooperation agreement and greater multilateral cooperation in the region with Cuba were reiterated in the 2012, 2013, and 2014 *INCSRs*.

U.S. Property Claims

An issue in the process of normalizing relations is Cuba's compensation for the expropriation of thousands of properties of U.S. companies and citizens in Cuba. The Foreign Claim Settlement Commission (FCSC), an independent agency within the Department of Justice, has certified 5,913 claims for expropriated U.S. properties in Cuba valued at $1.9 billion in two different claim programs; with interest, the value of the properties would be around $7 billion. In 1972, the FCSC certified 5,911 claims of U.S. citizens and companies that had their property confiscated by the Cuban government through April 1967, with 30 U.S. companies accounting for almost 60% of the claims.[129] In 2006, the FCSC certified two additional claims in a second claims program covering property confiscated after April 1967. Many of the companies that originally filed claims have been bought and sold numerous times. There are a variety of potential alternatives for restitution/compensation schemes to resolve the outstanding claims, but resolving the issue would likely entail considerable negotiation and cooperation between the two governments.[130]

The LIBERTAD Act (P.L. 104-114) includes the property claims issue as one of the many factors that the President needs to consider in determining when a transition government is in power in Cuba and when a democratically elected government is in power. These determinations are linked, respectively, to the suspension and termination of the economic embargo on Cuba. For a transition government, as set forth in Section 205(b)((2) of the law, the President shall take into account the extent to which the government has made public commitments and is making demonstrable progress in taking steps to return to U.S. citizens (and entities that are 50% or more beneficially owned by U.S. citizens) property taken by the Cuban government on or after January 1, 1959, or to provide equitable compensation for such property. A democratically elected government, as set forth in Section 206 of the law, is one that, among other conditions, has made demonstrable progress in returning such property or providing full compensation for such property in accordance with international law standards and practice.

Outlook

Although any change to the government's one-party communist political system appears unlikely, Cuba is moving toward a post-Castro era. Raúl

Castro has said that he would step down from power once his term of office is over in February 2018. Moreover, generational change in Cuba's governmental institutions has already begun. Under Raúl and beyond, the Cuban government is likely to continue its gradual economic policy changes, moving toward a more mixed economy with a stronger private sector, although it is uncertain whether the pace of reform will produce major improvements to the Cuban economy. The Obama Administration's major shift in U.S. policy toward Cuba is likely to open up engagement with the Cuban government in a variety of areas, including on the issue of U.S. property claims in Cuba dating back to the 1960s. Trade and travel linkages with Cuba will likely increase because of the policy changes, although to what extent is uncertain given that the overall embargo and numerous other sanctions against Cuba remain in place. The human rights situation in Cuba will likely remain a key U.S. concern. With diverse opinions in Congress over the Administration's policy shift, continued debate over many aspects of U.S. relations with Cuba will likely continue in the 114th Congress on such issues as the reestablishment of diplomatic relations, the designation of Cuba as a state sponsor of international terrorism, and U.S. economic sanctions on Cuba, especially on restrictions on travel and trade.

LEGISLATIVE INITIATIVES IN THE 114TH CONGRESS

H.R. 274 (Rush). United States-Cuba Normalization Act of 2015. The bill would remove provisions of law restricting trade and other relations with Cuba; authorize common carriers to install and repair telecommunications equipment and facilities in Cuba and otherwise provide telecommunications services between the United States and Cuba; prohibit restrictions on travel to and from Cuba and on transactions incident to such travel; direct the U.S. Postal Service to take actions to provide direct mail service to and from Cuba; call on the President to conduct negotiations with the government of Cuba to settle claims of U.S. nationals for the taking of property by the Cuban government and for securing the protection of internationally recognized human rights; extend nondiscriminatory trade treatment to the products of Cuba; prohibit limits on remittances to Cuba; and rescind the designation of the Cuban government as a state sponsor of international terrorism. Introduced January 12, 2015; referred to the Committee on Foreign Affairs, in addition to the Committees on Ways and Means, Energy and Commerce, Judiciary, Financial Services, Oversight and Government Reform, and Agriculture.

H.R. 403 (Rangel). Free Trade with Cuba Act. The bill would remove provisions of law restricting trade and other relations with Cuba; authorize common carriers to install and repair telecommunications equipment and facilities in Cuba and otherwise provide telecommunications services between the United States and Cuba; prohibit restrictions on travel to and from Cuba and on transactions incident to such travel; direct the U.S. Postal Service to take actions to provide direct mail service to and from Cuba; and call on the President to conduct negotiations with the government of Cuba to settle claims of U.S. nationals for the taking of property by the Cuban government and for securing the protection of internationally recognized human rights. Introduced January 16, 2015; referred to the Committee on Foreign Affairs, in addition to the Committees on Ways and Means, Energy and Commerce, the Judiciary, Financial Services, Oversight and Government Reform, and Agriculture.

H.R. 570 (McCollum). Stop Wasting Taxpayer Money on Cuba Broadcasting Act. The bill would repeal the Radio Broadcasting to Cuba Act (22 U.S.C. 1465 et seq.) and the Television Broadcasting to Cuba Act (22 U.S.C. 1464aa et seq.). Introduced January 27, 2015; referred to the Committee on Foreign Affairs.

H.R. 634 (Rangel). Export Freedom to Cuba Act of 2015. The bill would provide that travel to and from Cuba by U.S. citizens and residents, and any transactions incident to such travel, shall not be regulated or prohibited. Introduced February 2, 2015; referred to the House Committee on Foreign Affairs.

H.R. 635 (Rangel). Promoting American Agricultural and Medical Exports to Cuba Act of 2015. Among its provisions, the bill would permanently redefine the term "payment of cash in advance" to mean that payment is received before the transfer of title and release and control of the commodity to the purchaser; authorize direct transfers between Cuban and U.S. financial institutions for products exported under the terms of TSRA; establish an export promotion program for U.S. agricultural exports to Cuba; permit non-immigrant visas for Cuban nationals for activities related to purchasing U.S. agricultural goods; repeal a trademark sanction related to Cuba in a FY1999 omnibus appropriations measure (§211 of Division A, Title II, P.L. 105-277); prohibit restrictions on travel to Cuba; and repeal the onsite verification requirement for medical exports to Cuba under the CDA. Introduced February 2, 2015; referred to the Committee on Foreign Affairs, in addition to the Committees on Ways and Means, the Judiciary, Agriculture, and Financial Services.

H.R. 654 (Jolly). Naval Station Guantanamo Bay Protection Act. The bill would prohibit the modification, termination, abandonment, or transfer of the lease by which the United States acquired the land and waters containing Naval Station, Guantanamo Bay, Cuba, unless the President notifies Congress before, and after such notification, Congress enacts a law authorizing that modification, termination, abandonment, or transfer. Introduced February 2, 2015; referred to the Committee on Foreign Affairs.

H.R. 664 (Sanford). Freedom to Travel to Cuba Act of 2015. The bill would prohibit the President from prohibiting or regulating travel to or from Cuba by U.S. citizens or legal residents, or any of the transactions incident to such travel, including banking transactions. Introduced February 2, 2015; referred to the Committee on Foreign Affairs.

H.R. 735 (Serrano). Cuba Reconciliation Act. The bill, among its provisions, would lift the trade embargo on Cuba. It would remove provisions of law restricting trade and other relations with Cuba; authorize common carriers to install and repair telecommunications equipment and facilities in Cuba and otherwise provide telecommunications services between the United States and Cuba; prohibit restrictions on travel to and from Cuba and on transactions incident to such travel; and direct the U.S. Postal Service to take actions to provide direct mail service to and from Cuba. Introduced February 4, 2015; referred to the Committee on Foreign Affairs, in addition to the Committees on Ways and Means, Energy and Commerce, Financial Services, the Judiciary, Oversight and Government Reform, and Agriculture.

H.R. 738 (Serrano). Baseball Diplomacy Act. The bill would waive certain prohibitions with respect to nationals of Cuba coming to the United States to play organized professional baseball. Introduced February 4, 2015; referred to the Committee on Foreign Affairs, in addition to the Committee on the Judiciary.

S.Res. 26 (Durbin). The resolution would commend Pope Francis for his leadership in helping to secure the release of Alan Gross and for working with the Governments of the United States and Cuba to achieve a more positive relationship. Introduced January 13, 2015; referred to the Committee on Foreign Relations.

S. 299 (Flake). Freedom to Travel to Cuba Act of 2015. The bill would prohibit the President from regulating travel to or from Cuba by U.S. citizens or legal residents, or any of the transactions incident to such travel, including banking transactions. Introduced January 29, 2015; referred to the Committee on Foreign Relations.

S. 491 (Klobuchar). Freedom to Export to Cuba Act of 2015. The bill would remove many provisions of law restricting trade and other relations with Cuba, including certain restrictions in the CDA and TSRA. Introduced February 12, 2015; referred to the Committee on Banking, Housing, and Urban Affairs.

End Notes

[1] Portions of this background are drawn from U.S. Department of State, "Background Note: Cuba," April 28, 2011. For further background, see Rex A. Hudson, ed., *Cuba, A Country Study*, Federal Research Division, Library of Congress (Washington, DC: U.S. Government Publishing Office [GPO], 2002); "Country Profile: Cuba," Federal Research Division, Library of Congress, September 2006, available at http://lcweb2.loc.gov/frd/cs/profiles /Cuba.pdf; Leslie Bethell, ed., *Cuba, A Short History* (Cambridge, UK: Cambridge University Press, 1993); and Hugh Thomas, *Cuba: The Pursuit of Freedom* (New York: Harper & Row, Publishers, 1971).

[2] U.S. Senator Orville Platt introduced an amendment to an army appropriation bill that was approved by both houses and enacted into law in 1901.

[3] For more on Cuba's political succession, see CRS Report RS22742, *Cuba's Political Succession: From Fidel to Raúl Castro*. For background discussion of potential Cuban political scenarios envisioned in the aftermath of Fidel Castro's stepping down from power in 2006, see CRS Report RL33622, *Cuba's Future Political Scenarios and U.S. Policy Approaches*.

[4] Juan O. Tamayo, "Cuban Communists OK Term Limits for Party and Government Officials," *Miami Herald*, January 29, 2012, and "Cuba's Communists Meet to Update Party, Not Much Buzz on Street," *Miami Herald*, January 28, 2012; Patricia Grogg, "Cuba: Party Aims for Efficient, Inclusive Socialism," Inter Press Service, February 1, 2012.

[5] Damien Cave and Victoria Burnett, "As Castro Era Drifts to Close, a New Face Steps in at No. 2," *New York Times*, February 28, 2013; Marc Frank, "Castro Successor Lacks Charisma But Is Experienced Manager," Reuters, February 26, 2013.

[6] Tracy Wilkinson, "New Face Waits in Cuba," *Los Angeles Times*, February 7, 2015.

[7] Marc Frank, "Cuba's Raúl Castro Promises Succession Has Started," Reuters, July 26, 2013.

[8] Amnesty International, *Routine Repression, Political Short-Term Detentions and Harassment in Cuba*, March 2012.

[9] AI defines prisoners of conscience as those jailed because of their political, religious, or other conscientiously held beliefs; ethnic origin; sex; color; language; national or social origin; economic status; birth; sexual orientation or other status—provided they have neither used nor advocated violence.

[10] AI, "Prisoners of Conscience Released in Cuba," January 9, 2015.

[11] AI, "Government Critics Under House Arrest," December 15, 2014.

[12] Comisión Cubana de Derechos Humanos y Reconciliación Nacional (CCDHRN), "Lista Parcial de Sancionados o Procesados por Motivos Políticos en Cuba," June 23, 2014.

[13] Patricia Zengerle, "17 on Cuba Prisoner List Set Free Before U.S.-Havana Deal Announced," Reuters News, January 12, 2015.

[14] David Adams, Matt Spetalnick, and Lesley Wroughton, "How Prisoners Names Were Drawn Up in U.S.-Cuba Secret Talks," Reuters News, January 12, 2015.

[15] The additional prisoner on the list had already been freed conditionally on parole. The remaining 50 prisoners on the CCDHRN list included those convicted on a variety of charges that included hijacking, terrorism, sabotage, and espionage, although the UNPACU maintained that some of the remaining prisoners were peaceful political activists. See Adams, Spetalnick, and Wroughton, op. cit.

[16] CCDHRN, "Cuba: Algunos Actos de Represion Politica en el Mes de Enero de 2015," February 2, 2015.

[17] Sánchez's website, which has links to numerous other independent blogs and websites, is available at http://generacionyen.wordpress.com/.

[18] The website is available at http://www.14ymedio.com/.

[19] See http://www.palabranueva.net/newPage/index.php and http://www.espaciolaical.org/.

[20] Marc Frank, "Cuba's Catholic Church May Restrict Rare Forum for Open Debate," Reuters, June 16, 2014; Daniel Trotta and Rosa Tania Valdés, "Cuban Editors, Pressured to Leave Magazine, Announce New Venture," Reuters, July 1, 2014.

[21] Fabiola Santiago, "Despite 'Reforms" Some Cubans Aren't Free to Travel," *Miami Herald*, March 12, 2013; U.S. Department of State, "Cuban Compliance with the Migration Accords, (October 2013 to April 2014)," report to Congress, May 7, 2014.

[22] Information and statistics were drawn from several sources: U.S. Department of State, "U.S. Relations with Cuba," August 30, 2013; Economist Intelligence Unit, "Cuba Country Report," February 2013; Oficina Nacional de Estadísticas, "Anuario Estadístico de Cuba, 2011"; Marc Frank, "Cuban Sugar Out Tops Previous Harvest, But Well Below Plan," Reuters, May 19, 2014; and "Cuban Tourism Industry Stalls in 2013," Reuters, July 30, 2014.

[23] For example, see "Cuba, Economy, Seeking New Partners," *Latin American Caribbean & Central America Report*, May 2013.

[24] "Cuba Country Report," Economist Intelligence Unit (EIU), February 2015.

[25] Marc Frank, "Factbox—Key Political Risks to Watch in Cuba," Reuters News, May 13, 2013.

[26] Andrea Rodriguez and Anne Marie Garcia, "2 Years into Cuba's Free Market Experiment, Small Entrepreneurs Struggle to Stay Afloat," Associated Press, December 27, 2013; U.S. Department of State, "President Obama's New Cuba Policy Looks Forward, Not Back," U.S. Secretary of State John Kerry, Secretary of Commerce Penny Pritzker, and Treasury Secretary Jacob J. Lew, op-ed, *Miami Herald*, December 20, 2014.

[27] Michael Weissenstein and Andrea Rodriguez, "Raúl Castro Issues Stern Warning to Entrepreneurs Pushing Boundaries of Cuba's Economic Reforms," Associated Press, December 21, 2013.

[28] For more on Cuba's currency problem, see "Replacing Cuba's Dual Currency System: What Are the Issues That Really Matter?" *Latin American Economy & Business*, July 2013.

[29] U.S. Department of State, "Country Reports on Human Rights Practices for 2013, Cuba," February 27, 2014.

[30] "Cuba Country Report," EIU, February 2015.

[31] "Cuba: Exchange Rate Unification Approaching," *Latin America Regional Report: Caribbean & Central America*, March 2014.

[32] "Cuba Approves New Foreign Investment Law," *Latin American Regional Report: Caribbean & Central America*, April 2014; "What's Changed in Cuba's New Foreign Investment Law," Reuters News, March 29, 2014.

[33] Marc Frank, "Cuba Plans Big Tax Breaks to Lure Foreign Investors," Reuters News, March 26, 2014; and Daniel Trotta, "Cuba's Past Raises Skepticism About New Foreign Investment Law," Reuters News, March 31, 2014.

[34] "Cuba Seeks $8.7 Bn in Foreign Investment," EFE News Service, November 4, 2014.

[35] Marc Frank, "As Cuban Economy Stagnates, Economists Press for Deeper Reforms," Reuters News, October 24, 2014.

[36] Statistics drawn from Oficina Nacional de Estadística e Información, República de Cuba, Anuario Estadístico de Cuba 2013, Sector Externo, available at http://www.one.cu/aec2013 /esp/08_tabla_cuadro.htm.

[37] The BRICS is an association of five major emerging economies: Brazil, Russia, India, China, and South Africa.

[38] That agreement had been discussed in a 2013 visit by now Prime Minister Medvedev to Cuba, and had been announced in December 2013. Anna Andrianova and Bill Faries, "Russia Forgives $32B of Debt, Wants to Do Business in Cuba," Bloomberg News, July 13, 2014; Marc Frank, "Russia Signs Deal to Forgive $29 Billion of Cuba's Soviet-Era Debt – Diplomats," Reuters, December 9, 2013; "Castro Declares He Had a Good Visit with Russia's Medvedev," Agence France Presse, February 23, 2013.

[39] "Putin Denies Russia to Reopen Soviet-era Spy Post in Cuba," Reuters News, July 17, 2014.

[40] "Russia Cements Energy Ties with Latin America," *Oil Daily*, July 15, 2014.

[41] Marc Frank, "Chinese President Ends Regional Tour in Cradle of Cuban Revolution," Reuters News, July 23, 2014.

[42] "EU and Cuba Make Progress on Association Agreement," *Cuba Briefing* (a Caribbean Insight publication), September 4, 2014.

[43] European Union, Official Journal of the European Commission, "Common Position of 2 December 1996, defined by the Council on the Basis of Article J.2 of the Treaty on European Union, on Cuba," (96/697/CFSP), December 2, 1996.

[44] Anthony Boadle, "Cuban Doctors Tend to Brazil's Poor, Giving Rousseff a Boost," Reuters News, December 1, 2013.

[45] "UN Chief Pushes Cuba on 'Arbitrary Detentions,'" Agence France Presse, January 28, 2014.

[46] For further background, see section on "Cuba and the OAS" in archived CRS Report R40193, *Cuba: Issues for the 111th Congress*, by Mark P. Sullivan; also see CRS Report R42639, *Organization of American States: Background and Issues for Congress*, by Peter J. Meyer.

[47] United Nations Security Council, notes by the President of the Security Council, report of the panel of experts established pursuant to resolution 1874 (2009), S/1014/147, March 6, 2014, available at http://www.un.org/en/ga/ search/view_doc.asp?symbol=S/2014/147. The panel found that the "hidden cargo ... amounted to six trailers associated with surface-to-air missile systems and 25 shipping containers loaded with two disassembled MiG-21 aircraft, 15 engines for MiG-21 aircraft, components for surface-to-air missile systems, ammunition and miscellaneous arms-related material." According to the report, the "extraordinary and extensive efforts to conceal the cargo of arms and related material ... and the contingency instructions ... found onboard the vessel for preparing a false declaration for entering the Panama Canal ... point to a clear and conscious intention to circumvent the resolutions."

[48] U.N. Security Council, "Security Council Committee Designates Entity Subject to Measures Imposed by Resolution 1718 (2006)," press release, July 28, 2014.

[49] Michelle Nichols, "U.N. Blacklists Operator of North Korean Ship Seized in Panama," Reuters, July 29, 2014.

[50] For additional background, see archived CRS Report RL30386, *Cuba-U.S. Relations: Chronology of Key Events 1959-1999*, by Mark P. Sullivan.

[51] 27 *Federal Register* 1085, February 7, 1962 (Proclamation 3447, Embargo on All Trade with Cuba, February 3, 1962).

[52] In October 1960 under the Eisenhower Administration, exports to Cuba were strictly controlled under the authority of the Export Control Act of 1949 in response to the expropriation of U.S. properties. This in effect amounted to an embargo on exports of all products with the exception of certain foods, medicines, and medical supplies.

[53] 27 *Federal Register* 1116, February 7, 1962.

[54] 27 *Federal Register* 2765-2766, March 24, 1962.

[55] 28 *Federal Register* 6974-6985, July 9, 1963.

[56] 31 C.F.R. § 515.533.

[57] See especially 15 C.F.R. § 746.2 on Cuba, which refers to other parts of the EAR.

[58] Cuba's designation on the state sponsor of terrorism list has allowed U.S. nationals injured by an act of international terrorism to file lawsuits against Cuba in the United States for damages. For more information, see CRS Report WSLG254, *Can Victims of Terrorism in the United States Sue Foreign Governments?* by Jennifer K. Elsea.

[59] White House, "Remarks by the President at the Summit of the Americas Opening Ceremony," April 17, 2009.

[60] White House, Office of the Press Secretary, "Remarks by the President at a DSCC Fundraising Reception," Miami, Florida, November 8, 2013, available at http://www.whitehouse.gov /the-press-office/2013/11/08/remarks-presidentdscc-fundraising-reception-0.

[61] Adam Goldman and Missy Ryan, "Spy Helped Unmask 3 Cuban Spy Networks, U.S. Officials Say," *Washington Post*, December 18, 2014.

[62] White House, "Statement by the President on Cuba Policy Changes," December 17, 2014.

[63] U.S. Department of State, "Briefing on the Upcoming Migration and Reestablishment of Diplomatic Relations Talks with Cuba," January 19, 2015.

[64] U.S. Department of State, "Briefing on Changes in U.S. Policy Toward Cuba," December 18, 2014.

[65] The U.S. Interests Section in Havana also employs almost 400 foreign nationals. U.S. Department of State and Broadcasting Board of Governors, *Office of Inspector General, Inspection of U.S. Interests Section Havana, Cuba*, May 2014.

[66] Nick Miroff and Karen DeYoung, "Cuba Calls for Removal from U.S. Terror List," *Washington Post*, February 26, 2015.

[67] U.S. Department of State, "Background Briefing on Talks to Re-Establish Diplomatic Relations with Cuba," February 25, 2015.

[68] 80 *Federal Register* 2286-2302, January 16, 2015.

[69] On February 13, 2015, the State Department issued a list of eligible goods and services produced by independent Cuban entrepreneurs that may be imported. See http://www.state.gov/e/eb/tfs/spi/cuba/515582/237471.htm.

[70] Atlantic Council, Adrienne Arsht Latin American Center, *U.S-Cuba, A New Public Survey Supports Policy Change*, February 11, 2014, available at http://www.atlanticcouncil.org /publications/reports/us-cuba-a-new-public-surveysupports-policy-change.

[71] Florida International University, Cuban Research Institute, 2014 FIU Cuba Poll, *How Cuban Americans in Miami View U.S. Policies Toward Cuba*, June 17, 2014, available at https://cri.fiu.edu/news/2014/cuban-americans-favormore-nuanced-policy/2014-fiu-cuba-poll.pdf.

[72] As reported by PollingReport.com, available at http://www.pollingreport.com/cuba.htm.

[73] Scott Clement, "Poll: Support Increases for Lifting Cuba Embargo, Travel Restrictions," *Washington Post*, December 23, 2014.

[74] Also see CRS Report R43905, *Major Agricultural Trade Issues in the 114th Congress*, coordinated by Mark A. McMinimy.

[75] The U.S. trade statistics cited in this report are from the Department of Commerce, as presented by Global Trade Atlas.

[76] Juan Tamayo, "Big Drop in U.S. Agricultural Sales to Cuba," *Miami Herald*, July 29, 2010; Marc Frank, "U.S. Food Sales to Cuba Continued Decline in 2011," Reuters News, February 22, 2012; U.S.-Cuba Trade and Economic Council, Inc. "Economic Eye on Cuba," February 2015.

[77] University of Florida, Institute of Food and Agricultural Sciences, "Hot Topic Webinar – The Cuban Factor: Agricultural Trade with Cuba," presented by William Messina, Jr., February 4, 2015, available at http://www.piecenter.com/2015/01/28/hot-topic-webinar-the-cuban-factor-agricultural-trade-with-cuba/.

[78] USITC, *U.S. Agricultural Sales to Cuba: Certain Economic Effects of U.S. Restrictions*, USITC Publication 3932, July 2007, available at http://www.usitc.gov/publications /332/pub3932.pdf.

[79] USITC, *U.S. Agricultural Sales to Cuba: Certain Economic Effects of U.S. Restrictions, An Update*, Office of Industries Working Paper, by Jonathan R. Coleman, No. ID-22, June 2009, available at http://www.usitc.gov/publications/332/ID-22.pdf.

[80] USITC, "USITC to Study Economic Effects of U.S. Restrictions on Trade and Travel to Cuba," New Release 15- 011, January 30, 2015.

[81] For background information, see archived CRS Report RS21764, *Restricting Trademark Rights of Cubans: WTO Decision and Congressional Response*, by Margaret Mikyung Lee, March 9, 2004.

[82] For background, see archived CRS Report RL32014, *WTO Dispute Settlement: Status of U.S. Compliance in Pending Cases*, by Jeanne J. Grimmett, April 23, 2012.

[83] "U.S., EU Agree on Deadline for Complying with Section 211 WTO Finding," *Inside U.S. Trade*, April 12, 2002.

[84] World Trade Organization (WTO), "United States—Section 211 Omnibus Appropriations Act of 1998, Understanding Between the European Communities and the United States," WT/DC176/16, July 1, 2005; WTO, Dispute Settlement Body, "Minutes of Meeting, Held in the Centre William Rappard on 20 July 2005," WT/DSB/M/194, August 26, 2005; and "Japan, EU Suspend WTO Retaliation Against U.S. in Two Cases," *Inside U.S. Trade*, July 15, 2005.

[85] "EU, Cuba Spar with U.S. over 'Havana Club' Rum," Agence France Presse, June 25, 2013.

[86] "PTO Cancels Cuban 'Havana Club' Mark; Bacardi Set to Sell Rum Under Same Mark," *International Trade Daily*, August 10, 2006.

[87] "Pernod Ricard: Havana Club International Encouraged by Dissenting Opinion of Judge Silberman Will Seek Rehearing by Full Court of Appeals," *Business Wire*, March 29, 2011.

[88] "USA-Engage Joins Cuba Fight," *Cuba Trader*, April 1, 2002; the House Committee on the Judiciary held a March 3, 2010, hearing on the "Domestic and International Trademark Implications of HAVANA CLUB and Section 211 of the Omnibus Appropriations Act of 2009," which featured proponents of both legislative approaches.

[89] The U.S. Government Accountability Office (GAO) reports that Congress appropriated $205 million for Cuba democracy programs from FY1996 through FY2011. See U.S. GAO, *Cuba Democracy Assistance, USAID's Program Is Improved, But State Could Better Monitor Its Implementing Partners*, GAO-13-285, January 2013.

[90] U.S. Government Accountability Office (GAO), *U.S. Democracy Assistance for Cuba Needs Better Management and Oversight*, GAO-07-147, November 2006.

[91] Oscar Corral, "Federal Program to Help Democracy in Cuba Falls Short of Mark," *Miami Herald*, November 14, 2006, and "Is U.S. Aid Reaching Castro Foes?" *Miami Herald*, November 15, 2006.

[92] U.S. GAO, *Foreign Assistance: Continued Efforts Needed to Strengthen USAID's Oversight of U.S. Democracy Assistance for Cuba*, GAO-09-165, November 2008.

[93] U.S. GAO, *Cuba Democracy Assistance, USAID's Program Is Improved, But State Could Better Monitor Its Implementing Partners*, GAO-13-285, January 2013.

[94] Desmond Butler, Jack Gillum, and Alberto Arce, "U.S. Secretly Created 'Cuban Twitter' to Stir Unrest," Associated Press, April 3, 2014.

[95] USAID, "Statement in Reference to the Associated Press Article on "Cuba Twitter" on April 3, 2014," press statement, April 3, 2014; "Eight Facts About ZunZuneo," April 7, 2014, available at http://blog.usaid.gov/2014/04/ eight-facts-about-zunzuneo/.

[96] Desmond Butler, Jack Gillum, Alberto Arce, and Andrea Rodriguez, "The Big Story, U.S. Sent Latin Youth Undercover in Anti-Cuba Ploy," Associated Press, August 4, 2014.

[97] USAID, "Statement from USAID Spokesperson Matt Herrick on Cuba Civil Society Story," August 4, 2014.

[98] See the full text of the Broadcasting Board of Governors FY2015 budget request, available at http://www.bbg.gov/ wp-content/media/2014/03/FY-2015-BBG-Congressional-Budget-Request-FINAL-21-March-2014.pdf.

[99] See the following reports and audits from 1990 through 2008: U.S. General Accounting Office (GAO), *Broadcasts to Cuba, TV Marti Surveys Are Flawed*, GAO/NSIAD-90-252, August 1990; U.S. GAO, *TV Marti, Costs and Compliance with Broadcast Standards and International Agreements*, GAO/NSIAD-92-199, May 1992; U.S. GAO, letter to Hon. Howard L. Berman and Hon. John F. Kerry regarding Radio Marti broadcast standards, GAO/NSIAD-93-126R, February 17, 1993; Advisory Panel on Radio and TV Marti, *Report of the Advisory Panel on Radio and TV Marti*, three volumes, March 1994; U.S. GAO, *Radio Marti, Program Review Processes Need Strengthening*, GAO/NSIAD-94-265, September 1994; U.S. GAO, *U.S. Information Agency, Issues Related to Reinvention Planning in the Office of Cuba Broadcasting*, GAO/NSIAD-96-110, May 1996; U.S. Department of State, Office of the Inspector General, *Review of Policies and Procedures for Ensuring that Radio Marti Broadcasts Adhere to Applicable Requirements*, 99-IB-010, June 1999; U.S. Department of State and the Broadcasting Board of Governors, Office of Inspector General, *Review of the Effectiveness and Implementation of Office of Cuba Broadcasting's New Program Initiatives*, Report No. IBO-A03-01, January 2003, and *Report of Inspection, Office of Cuba Broadcasting,* Report No. ISP-IB 07-35, June 2007; and U.S. GAO, *Broadcasting to Cuba, Weaknesses in Contracting Practices Reduced Visibility into Selected Award Decisions*, GAO-08-764, July 2008.

[100] U.S. GAO, *Broadcasting to Cuba, Actions Are Needed to Improve Strategy and Operations*, GAO-09-127, January 2009.

[101] U.S. Congress, Senate Committee on Foreign Relations, *Cuba: Immediate Action Is Needed to Ensure the Survivability of Radio and TV Marti*, committee print, 111th Cong., 2nd sess., April 29, 2010, S.Prt. 111-46 (Washington: GPO, 2010).

[102] U.S. Government Accountability Office, *Broadcasting Board of Governors Should Provide Additional Information to Congress Regarding Broadcasting to Cuba*, December 13, 2011, available at http://www.gao.gov/assets/590/ 586869.pdf.

[103] For background information, see archived CRS Report RL32251, *Cuba and the State Sponsors of Terrorism List*, by Mark P. Sullivan, August 22, 2006.

[104] Section 40 of the AECA, as enacted in 1986, made any government subject to Section 6(j) of the EAA also subject to AECA-related sanctions.

[105] U.S. Department of State, *Country Reports on Terrorism 2013*, April 30, 2014.

[106] U.S. Department of State, *Country Reports on Terrorism 2007*, April 30, 2008.

[107] FBI, Most Wanted Terrorists, Joanne Deborah Chesimard, poster, at http://www.fbi.gov/wanted/wanted_terrorists/ joanne-deborah-chesimard/view.

[108] For example, see the U.S. Attorney's Office, Southern District of Florida, "Thirty-Three Defendants Charged in Staged Automobile Accident Scheme," press release, May 16, 2013; "Experts: Florida Couple May Not Be Welcome in Cuba," *Naples Daily News*, April 9, 2013; and Jay Weaver, "FBI Struggling to Catch Dozens of Fraud Fugitives Hiding in Cuba," *Miami Herald*, July 16, 2011.

[109] On July 17, 2014, Potts was sentenced to 20 years in jail by a U.S. federal judge in Florida. See Zachary Fagenson, "Ex-Black Panther Sentenced to 20 Years for 1980s Hijacking," Reuters, July 17, 2014.

[110] George Mast, "Murder Suspects Caught in Cuba," *Courier-Post* (New Jersey), September 30, 2011.

[111] Paul Haven and Peter Orsi, "Cuba Says It Will Give U.S. Florida Couple Who Allegedly Kidnapped Children," Associated Press, April 9, 2013.

[112] For more background on Posada, see CRS Report RS21049, *Latin America: Terrorism Issues*, *Latin America: Terrorism Issues*.

[113] Also see CRS Report IN10204, *U.S. Policy on Cuban Migration*, by Andorra Bruno and Ruth Ellen Wasem and CRS Report R40566, *Cuban Migration to the United States: Policy and Trends*, by Ruth Ellen Wasem.

[114] Alfonso Chardy and Juan Tamayo, "Exodus of Cubans Slowing," *Miami Herald*, October 6, 2010. U.S. Department of State, "Cuban Compliance with the Migration Accords (April 2012 to October 2012)," report to Congress, October 22, 2012.

[115] U.S. Coast Guard, Alien Migrant Interdiction, Coast Guard Office of Law Enforcement, "Total Interdictions, Fiscal Year 1982 to Present," December 31, 2014.

[116] Alfonso Chardy and Juan O. Tamayo, "Illegal Cuban Migration, After Years of Decline, Is Up Again," Miami Herald, *Miami Herald*, October 8, 2011; Alfonso Chardy and Juan O. Tamayo, "Number of Cubans Trying to Enter U.S. Increases," *Miami Herald*, June 17, 2012.

[117] U.S. Department of State, "Cuban Compliance with the Migration Accords, (October 2013 to April 2014)," report to Congress, May 7, 2014, and "Cuban Compliance with the Migration Accords, (April to October 2014)," report to Congress, November 6, 2014.

[118] U.S. Department of State, "Cuban Compliance with the Migration Accords, (April to October 2014)," report to Congress, November 6, 2014.

[119] Nick Miroff, "Anxious Cubans Head for U.S. Soil," *Washington Post*, January 28, 2015; Alfonso Chardy, "Cuban Migrants Flow into South Florida at Highest Rate in 10 Years," *Miami Herald*, February 1, 2015.

[120] U.S. Department of State, "Migration Talks with Cuba," January 22, 2015.

[121] República de Cuba, Ministerio de Relaciones Exteriores, "Declaración de la Jefa de la Delegación de Cuba a Ronda Migratoria con Estados Unidos," January 21, 2015.

[122] "An Open Letter Concerning Illegal Migration into the United States," Department of Homeland Security documents, January 21, 2015; "U.S., Cuba Agree to Disagree About Migration," EFE News Service, January 21, 2015.

[123] U.S. Department of State, "Cuban Compliance with the Migration Accords, (April to October 2014)," report to Congress, November 6, 2014.

[124] Mimi Whitfield, "U.S. Begins New Multiple-Entry Visa Program for Cuban Visitors," *Miami Herald*, August 1, 2013; Marc Frank, "Cubans Welcome New U.S. Visa Policy, Government Largely Silent," Reuters News, August 2, 2013; and U.S. Department of State, United States Interest Section, Havana, Cuba, "Important Notice: Increase in B-2 Visa Validity," available at http://havana.usint.gov/visa_appointment_information.html.

[125] David Adams and Tom Brown, "Cuban Perks Under Scrutiny in U.S. Immigration Reform," Reuters News, February 8, 2013; Stephen Johnson "Recommendations for the New Administration: Interests, Policies, and Challenges in the Americas," Center for Strategic and International Studies, November 21, 2012; and Philip Peters, "Migration Policy Reform: Cuba Gets Started, U.S. Should Follow," Lexington Institute, December 2012.

[126] Marc R. Rosenblum and Faye Hipsman, "Normalization of Relations with Cuba May Portend Changes to U.S. Immigration Policy," Migration Policy Institute, January 13, 2015.

[127] Lizette Alvarez, "Law Favoring Cuban Arrivals Is Challenged," *New York Times*, February 2, 2015.

[128] On March 12, 2002, Cuba's Ministry of Foreign Affairs and the Cuban Interests Section in Washington delivered three diplomatic notes to the U.S. Interests Section in Havana and the State Department in Washington proposing agreements on drug interdiction, terrorism, and migration issues. See "Statement from the Ministry of Foreign Affairs: Prominent Drug Trafficker Arrested in Our Country," Information Office, Cuban Interests Section, March 17, 2002; "Cuba Offers to Sign Anti-Drug Pact," *Miami Herald*, April 8, 2006.

[129] "A Road Map for Restructuring Future U.S. Relations with Cuba," policy paper, Atlantic Council, June 1995, Appendix D.

[130] Matías F. Travieso-Díaz, "Alternative Recommendations for Dealing with Expropriated U.S. Property in Post-Castro Cuba," in *Cuba in Transition, Volume 12*, Association for the Study of the Cuban Economy, 2002.

In: Cuba in Context
Editor: Janet G. Campbell
ISBN: 978-1-63482-985-4

Chapter 2

CUBA SANCTIONS: LEGISLATIVE RESTRICTIONS LIMITING THE NORMALIZATION OF RELATIONS*

Dianne E. Rennack and Mark P. Sullivan

SUMMARY

In December 2014, President Obama announced major changes in U.S. policy toward Cuba, including the restoration of diplomatic relations (relations were severed in January 1961), a review by the Department of State of Cuba's designation as a state sponsor of terrorism (Cuba was designated in 1982), and an increase in travel, trade, and the free flow of information to Cuba. This third step required the Departments of Commerce and the Treasury to amend the embargo regulations, which were announced on January 15, 2015.

When the President announced his policy change on Cuba, he acknowledged that he does not have authority to lift the embargo because it is codified in legislation. While the embargo was first imposed in the early 1960s under the authority of the Foreign Assistance Act of 1961 and the Trading with the Enemy Act, Congress enacted additional laws over the years that strengthened the embargo on Cuba, including the Cuban Democracy Act of 1992, the Cuban Liberty and Democratic Solidarity

* This is an edited, reformatted and augmented version of a Congressional Research Service publication R43888, prepared for Members and Committees of Congress, dated February 13, 2015.

Act (LIBERTAD) Act of 1996 (which codified the embargo regulations), and the Trade Sanctions Reform and Export Enhancement Act of 2000. Congress also has enacted numerous other provisions of law that impose sanctions on Cuba, including restrictions on trade, foreign aid, and support from the international financial institutions.

This report provides information on legislative provisions restricting relations with Cuba. It lists the various provisions of law comprising economic sanctions on Cuba, including key laws that are the statutory basis of the embargo, and provides information on the authority to lift or waive these restrictions.

INTRODUCTION

Since the early 1960s, U.S. policy toward Cuba has consisted largely of isolating the island nation through comprehensive economic sanctions, including an embargo on trade and financial transactions. President John F. Kennedy proclaimed an embargo on trade between the United States and Cuba in February 1962,[1] citing Section 620(a) of the Foreign Assistance Act of 1961 (FAA), which authorizes the President "to establish and maintain a total embargo upon all trade between the United States and Cuba."[2] At the same time, the Department of the Treasury issued the Cuban Import Regulations to deny the importation into the United States of all goods imported from or through Cuba.[3] The authority for the embargo was later expanded in March 1962 to include the Trading with the Enemy Act (TWEA).[4]

In July 1963, the Treasury Department revoked the Cuban Import Regulations and replaced them with the more comprehensive Cuban Assets Control Regulations (CACR)—31 C.F.R. Part 515 under the authority of TWEA and Section 620(a) of the FAA.[5] The CACR, which include a prohibition on most financial transactions with Cuba and a freeze of Cuban government assets in the United States, remain the main body of Cuba embargo regulations, and have been amended many times over the years to reflect changes in policy. They are administered by the Treasury Department's Office of Foreign Assets Control (OFAC), and prohibit financial transactions as well as trade transactions with Cuba. The CACR also require that all exports to Cuba be licensed by the Department of Commerce, Bureau of Industry and Security, under the provisions of the Export Administration Act of 1979, as amended.[6] The Export Administration Regulations (EAR) are found at 15 C.F.R. Sections 730-774.[7]

Congress subsequently strengthened sanctions on Cuba through provisions in such legislation as the Cuban Democracy Act of 1992 (CDA, P.L. 102-484, Title XVII), the Cuban Liberty and Democratic Solidarity (LIBERTAD) Act of 1996 (P.L. 104-114), and the Trade Sanctions Reform and Export Enhancement Act of 2000 (TSRA, P.L. 106-387, Title IX).

- Among its sanctions, the CDA prohibits U.S. subsidiaries from engaging in trade with Cuba and prohibits entry into the United States for any sea-borne vessel to load or unload freight if it has been involved in trade with Cuba within the previous 180 days.
- The LIBERTAD Act codified the economic embargo, including all restrictions under the CACR, although the President retains broad authority to amend the regulations. Nevertheless, as set forth in the LIBERTAD Act, the President cannot eliminate the embargo regulations without making a determination that a transition government is in power in Cuba. The LIBERTAD Act also requires the President to end the embargo if he determines that a democratically elected government is in power.
- While TSRA authorizes U.S. commercial exports to Cuba, it also includes prohibitions on U.S. assistance and financing and requires "payment of cash in advance" or third-country financing for the exports. The act also prohibits tourist travel to Cuba.

In addition to these key acts that constitute the economic embargo, there are numerous other provisions of law that impose sanctions on Cuba, including restrictions on trade, foreign aid, and support from international financial institutions. The government of Cuba also was designated by the State Department as a state sponsor of international terrorism in 1982 under Section 6(j) of the Export Administration Act and other laws because of its alleged ties to international terrorism.[8]

On December 17, 2014, President Barack Obama announced major changes in policy toward Cuba, including the intention to reestablish diplomatic relations that were severed in 1961, a review of Cuba's designation as a state sponsor of international terrorism, and numerous policy measures to increase travel, commerce, and the free flow of information to Cuba. To implement this last step, the Departments of the Treasury and Commerce issued amendments to the CACR[9] and EAR to enter into effect on January 16, 2015, that significantly eased the embargo in such areas as travel, remittances, trade (including consumer communication devices and certain goods and services for the private sector), and financial services (permitting U.S. correspondent bank accounts in Cuban financial institutions).[10]

When announcing the policy changes, the President acknowledged that he does not have the authority to lift the embargo, but maintained that he looks forward to engaging Congress in a debate about doing so. Without a presidential determination required by the LIBERTAD Act that Cuba has a democratically elected government in place, congressional action would be required to end the embargo by amending or repealing the LIBERTAD and other embargo-related statutes.[11]

This report provides information on legislative provisions restricting relations with Cuba. *Table 1* lists the various provisions of law comprising economic sanctions on Cuba, including key laws that are the statutory basis of the embargo, and provides information on the authority to lift or waive the restrictions.

Table 1. Legislative Restrictions Limiting the Normalization of U.S.-Cuban Relations

Statutory Basis	Restriction	Authority to Lift or Waive
Key Restrictions that Form the Core of the U.S. Economic Sanctions Regime on Cuba: The Embargo		
Sec. 620(a)(1), Foreign Assistance Act of 1961 (22 U.S.C. 2370(a)(1))	Prohibits foreign aid "to the present government of Cuba." Authorizes the President "to establish and maintain a total embargo upon all trade between the United States and Cuba."	The prohibition on aid has no waiver, though could be overridden by appropriations language that provides aid "notwithstanding any other provision of law." As set forth in the law, the total embargo is a discretionary authorization. Sec. 204, Cuban Liberty and Democratic Solidarity (LIBERTAD) Act (22 U.S.C. 6064), however, authorizes the President to suspend the enforcement of sec. 620(a) only if he determines "a transition government is in power in Cuba." Sec. 204 of that Act, furthermore, requires the President to terminate sanctions under sec. 620(a) and other measures if he determines

Statutory Basis	Restriction	Authority to Lift or Waive
		that "a democratically elected government in Cuba is in power." Sec. 204(d)(1) of that Act repeals sec. 620(a) on President making such a determination.
Sec. 620(a)(2), Foreign Assistance Act of 1961 (22U.S.C. 2370(a)(2))	Authorizes the President to prohibit foreign aid to "any government of Cuba." Denies Cuba a quota for sugar trade, "or to receive any other benefit under any law of the United States....	As set forth in the law, the prohibitions on aid and sugar imports are discretionary, "except as may be deemed necessary by the President in the interests of the United States." Sec. 204, Cuban Liberty and Democratic Solidarity (LIBERTAD) Act (22 U.S.C. 6064), however, authorizes the President to suspend the enforcement of sec. 620(a) only if he determines "a transition government is in power in Cuba." Sec. 204, furthermore, requires the President to terminate sanctions under sec. 620(a) and other measures if he determines that "a democratically elected government in Cuba is in power." Sec. 204(d)(1) of that Act repeals sec. 620(a) on President making such a determination.
Sec. 5(b), Trading With the Enemy Act (50 U.S.C. App. 5(b))	Authorizes the President to restrict or prohibit trade, transactions, and access to assets and property.	The Cuban Assets Control Regulations, 31 CFR Part 515, were issued in July 1963 under the authority of TWEA. Pursuant to the law, the President may terminate the national emergency and restrictions under TWEA at any time. Sec. 204, Cuban Liberty and Democratic Solidarity (LIBERTAD) Act (22 U.S.C. 6064), however, authorizes the President to suspend the enforcement of 31 CFR Part 515 only if he determines that "a transition government is in power

Table 1. (Continued)

Statutory Basis	Restriction	Authority to Lift or Waive
		in Cuba." Sec. 204, furthermore, requires the President to terminate the economic embargo of Cuba, including the restrictions under 31 CFR Part 515 if he determines that "a democratically elected government in Cuba is in power." Nevertheless, the Secretary of the Treasury retains authority to amend regulations therein, in accordance with 31 CFR Part 515. 201, which, in part, provides: "All of the following transactions are prohibited, except as specifically authorized by the Secretary of the Treasury.... "
Sec. 1704, Cuban Democracy Act of 1992 (22 U.S.C. 6003)	Authorizes the President to prohibit foreign aid under the Foreign Assistance Act of 1961, transactions under the Arms Export Control Act, or debt forgiveness, to any third country providing assistance to Cuba.	As set forth in the law, the prohibitions are at the President's discretion. Sec. 204, Cuban Liberty and Democratic Solidarity (LIBERTAD) Act (22 U.S.C. 6064), however, authorizes the President to suspend the enforcement of sec. 1704 only if he determines that "a transition government is in power in Cuba." Sec. 204, furthermore, requires the President to terminate sanctions under sec. 1704 and other measures if he determines that "a democratically elected government in Cuba is in power." Sec. 204(d)(1) of that Act repeals sec. 1704 on President making such a determination.
Sec. 1705(d), Cuban Democracy Act of 1992 (22 U.S.C. 6004(d))	Requires on-site verification for the export of medicines and medical supplies (unless the recipient is a nongovernmental	The President is required to determine that the U.S. government can verify the end use of such exports.

Statutory Basis	Restriction	Authority to Lift or Waive
	organization receiving donations).	Sec. 204, Cuban Liberty and Democratic Solidarity (LIBERTAD) Act (22 U.S.C. 6064) authorizes the President to suspend the enforcement of sec. 1705(d) only if he determines that "a transition government is in power in Cuba." Sec. 204, furthermore, requires the President to terminate sanctions under sec. 1705 and other measures if he determines that "a democratically elected government in Cuba is in power." Sec. 204(d)(1) of that Act repeals sec. 1705(d) on President making such a determination.
Sec. 1705(e)(5), Cuban Democracy Act of 1992 (22 U.S.C. 6004(e)(5))	Sec. 1705, overall, authorizes "support for the Cuban people," including allowing telecommunications services between the United States and Cuba. Sec. 1705(e)(5), however, clarifies that this allowance does not authorize a U.S. person to invest in Cuba's domestic telecommunications network.	
Sec. 1706(a), Cuban Democracy Act of 1992 (22 U.S.C. 6005(a))	Prohibits specific licenses for transactions relating to trade between Cuba and U.S.-owned or -controlled companies in third countries "in appropriate cases," codifying requirements stated in 31 CFR Part 515.559 as of July 1, 1989 (effective October 23, 1992).	Sec. 1708 provides that the President may waive if he determines that the government of Cuba (1) has held free and fair elections, (2) permits opposition parties to participate, (3) respects "basic civil liberties and human rights of the citizens of Cuba," (4) is moving toward a free market economy, and (5) is committed to constitutional change that ensures regular free and fair elections. Sec. 204, Cuban Liberty and Democratic Solidarity (LIBERTAD) Act (22 U.S.C.

Table 1. (Continued)

Statutory Basis	Restriction	Authority to Lift or Waive
		6064), however, authorizes the President to suspend the enforcement of sec. 1706 only if he determines that "a transition government is in power in Cuba." Sec. 204, furthermore, requires the President to terminate sanctions under sec. 1706 and other measures if he determines that "a democratically elected government in Cuba is in power." Sec. 204(d)(1) of that Act repeals sec. 1706 on President making such a determination.
Sec. 1706(b), Cuban Democracy Act of 1992 (22 U.S.C. 6005(b))	Prohibits entry into U.S. ports by any vessel that has entered a Cuban port in the previous 180 days. Prohibits entry into U.S. ports by any vessel carrying goods or passengers to or from Cuba in which Cuba or a Cuban national has any interest. Prohibits the use of a general license for ship stores for any vessel carrying goods or passengers to or from Cuba in which Cuba or a Cuban national has any interes	Licenses may be issued at the discretion of the Secretary of the Treasury. Sec. 1708 provides that the President may waive if he determines that the government of Cuba (1) has held free and fair elections, (2) permits opposition parties to participate, (3) respects "basic civil liberties and human rights of the citizens of Cuba," (4) is moving toward a free market economy, and (5) is committed to constitutional change that ensures regular free and fair elections. Sec. 204, Cuban Liberty and Democratic Solidarity (LIBERTAD) Act (22 U.S.C. 6064), however, authorizes the President to suspend the enforcement of sec. 1706 only if he determines that "a transition government is in power in Cuba." Sec. 204, furthermore, requires the President to terminate sanctions under sec. 1706 and other measures if he determines that "a democratically elected government

Statutory Basis	Restriction	Authority to Lift or Waive
		in Cuba is in power." Sec. 204(d)(1) of that Act repeals sec. 1706 on President making such a determination.
Sec. 1706(c), Cuban Democracy Act of 1992 (22 U.S.C. 6005(c))	Requires the President to "establish strict limits on remittances to Cuba by United States persons for the purpose of financing the travel of Cubans to the United States.... "	The term "strict limits" is undefined, so left to the discretion of the President. Sec. 1708 provides that the President may waive if he determines that the government of Cuba (1) has held free and fair elections, (2) permits opposition parties to participate, (3) respects "basic civil liberties and human rights of the citizens of Cuba," (4) is moving toward a free market economy, and (5) is committed to constitutional change that ensures regular free and fair elections. Sec. 204, Cuban Liberty and Democratic Solidarity (LIBERTAD) Act (22 U.S.C. 6064), however, authorizes the President to suspend the enforcement of sec. 1706 only if he determines that "a transition government is in power in Cuba." Sec. 204, furthermore, requires the President to terminate sanctions under sec. 1706 and other measures if he determines that "a democratically elected government in Cuba is in power." Sec. 204(d)(1) of that Act repeals sec. 1706 on President making such a determination.
Sec. 102(h), Cuban Liberty and Democratic Solidarity (LIBERTAD) Act of 1996 (22 U.S.C. 6032(h))	Codifies the economic embargo as in effect on March 1, 1996, including restrictions stated in regulations at 31 CFR Part 515.	Within 31 CFR Part 515, the Secretary of the Treasury retains authority to amend regulations therein, in accordance with 31 CFR Part 515. 201, which, in part, provides: "All of the following transactions are prohibited, except as specifically authorized by the

Table 1. (Continued)

Statutory Basis	Restriction	Authority to Lift or Waive
		Secretary of the Treasury.... " Sec. 204, Cuban Liberty and Democratic Solidarity (LIBERTAD) Act (22 U.S.C. 6064) authorizes the President to suspend the enforcement of 31 CFR Part 515 only if he determines that "a transition government is in power in Cuba." Sec. 204, furthermore, requires the President to terminate the economic embargo of Cuba, including the restrictions under 31 CFR Part 515, if he determines that "a democratically elected government in Cuba is in power."
Sec. 103(a), Cuban Liberty and Democratic Solidarity (LIBERTAD) Act of 1996 (22 U.S.C. 6033(a))	Prohibits a U.S. person or entity from financing any transaction that involves confiscated property in Cuba where the claim is owned by a U.S. national.	Sec. 103(b) provides that the President may suspend if he determines a transition government is in power; he may terminate if the transition to democracy is met as stated in secs. 203 and 204.
Sec. 104(a), Cuban Liberty and Democratic Solidarity (LIBERTAD) Act of 1996 (22 U.S.C. 6034(a))	Requires the Secretary of the Treasury to instruct U.S. executive directors to the international financial institutions to oppose Cuba's admission to such institution.	The President may suspend if he determines a democratically elected government is in power. The President may encourage membership, and the Secretary of the Treasury may encourage loans and assistance, when a transition government is in power, "to contribute to a stable foundation for a democratically elected government in Cuba."
Sec. 104(b), Cuban Liberty and Democratic Solidarity (LIBERTAD) Act of 1996 (22 U.S.C. 6034(b))	Requires the Secretary of the Treasury to withhold U.S. payment to any international financial institution in an amount equal to that institution's loan or assistance to Cuba if that loan is opposed by the United States.	The statute requires the United States to oppose Cuba's membership (in sec. 104(a)); it does not require opposing any loan or program of an international financial institution. If the United States supports a program or abstains from a vote, this

Statutory Basis	Restriction	Authority to Lift or Waive
		requirement would be inapplicable. Only if the United States opposes a loan would proportionate withholding be required.
Sec. 111(b), Cuban Liberty and Democratic Solidarity (LIBERTAD) Act of 1996 (22 U.S.C. 6041(b))	Requires withholding some foreign aid to any third country in amounts equal to that country's aid to Cuba to complete its nuclear facility at Juragua.	No waiver; however the statute allows aid to continue for humanitarian needs, disaster relief, refugee relief, democracy, rule of law, private sector and NGO development, free market economy development, nonproliferation, and secondary school exchanges.
Title III, Cuban Liberty and Democratic Solidarity (LIBERTAD) Act of 1996 (22 U.S.C. 6081-6085)	Allow U.S. nationals whose property was confiscated by the Cuban government a right of action to seek compensation in U.S. federal court from those who "traffic" in such property.	The President may suspend the right of action for successive 6-month periods if he determines that such suspension is in the U.S. national interest and will expedite Cuba's transition to democracy. The President has exercised this suspension since the law's enactment. Sec. 204 of the Act also authorizes the President, once he determines that a transition government is in power, to suspend the right of action under title III to the extent that it contributes to a stable foundation for a democratically elected government in Cuba.
Title IV, Cuban Liberty and Democratic Solidarity (LIBERTAD) Act of 1996 (22 U.S.C. 6091)	Requires the Secretary of State and Attorney General to deny entry into the United States to any person (or family member of that person) who has confiscated property, or has been involved in a related transaction, to which a U.S. person has a claim.	Secretary of State may, case-by-case, allow entry into the United States for medical purposes or to attend to litigation actions under title III of the Act (relating to protection of property rights of U.S. nationals).
Sec. 906, Trade Sanctions and Export Enhancement Act of	Exports of agricultural commodities, medicine, and medical supplies to Cuba	No waiver.

Table 1. (Continued)

Statutory Basis	Restriction	Authority to Lift or Waive
2000 (22 U.S.C. 7205)	require a 1-year license and 1-year contract.	
Sec. 908, Trade Sanctions and Export Enhancement Act of 2000 (22 U.S.C. 7207)	Prohibits U.S. aid for exports to Cuba. Limits the means by which a U.S. person may finance the sale of agricultural products to Cuba to cash in advance or third-country financing.	No waiver.
Sec. 910(b), Trade Sanctions and Export Enhancement Act of 2000 (22 U.S.C. 7208(b))	The Secretary of the Treasury may not authorize travel-related transactions listed in paragraph (c) of section 515.560 of title 31, Code of Federal Regulations, either by a general license or on a case-by-case basis by a specific license for travel to, from, or within Cuba for tourist activities.	No waiver.
Sec. 620A, Foreign Assistance Act of 1961 (22 U.S.C. 2371)	Prohibits funding under the Foreign Assistance Act of 1961, Agricultural Trade Development and Assistance Act of 1954, Peace Corps Act, and Export-Import Bank Act of 1945, to any country the government of which the Secretary of State finds "has repeatedly provided support for acts of international terrorism."	President may lift restrictions if he determines (1) "there has been a fundamental change in the leadership and policies of the government," (2) the government does not support acts of international terrorism, and (3) the government provides assurances that it will not support international terrorism in the future. Alternatively, the President may lift restrictions if he determines that the government has not supported terrorism in the preceding six months, and has provided assurances that it will not support international terrorism in the future. The President may waive if he determines it is in U.S. national security interests or that

Statutory Basis	Restriction	Authority to Lift or Waive
		humanitarian reasons (for non-lethal aid) justify a waiver.
Sec. 40, Arms Export Control Act (22 U.S.C. 2780)	Prohibits transactions relating to providing, directly or indirectly, any munitions acquisition to any country the government of which the Secretary of State finds "has repeatedly provided support for acts of international terrorism." U.S. persons are prohibited from exporting, selling, leasing, loaning, granting, providing, or facilitating the acquisition of any munitions item to/by Cuba.	The Secretary of State may waive some prohibitions if he determines, after consulting Congress, that "unusual and compelling circumstances require" it. President may lift restrictions if he determines that (1) "there has been a fundamental change in the leadership and policies of the government," (2) the government does not support acts of international terrorism, and (3) the government provides assurances that it will not support international terrorism in the future. Alternatively, the President may lift restrictions if he determines that the government has not supported terrorism in the preceding six months, and has provided assurances that it will not support international terrorism in the future. The President may waive for a specific transaction if he determines it is "essential to the national security of the United States" and consults with and reports to Congress. Congress may block lifting this restriction by passing a joint resolution.
Sec. 6(j), Export Administration Act of 1979 (50 U.S.C. App. 2405(j))	Requires a validated export license, with a presumption of denial for such issuance, to any country the government of which has repeatedly provided support for acts of international terrorism.	The Secretary of State may issue licenses with prior notification to Congress. President may lift restrictions if he determines that (1) "there has been a fundamental change in the leadership and policies of the government," (2) the government

Table 1. (Continued)

Statutory Basis	Restriction	Authority to Lift or Waive
		does not support acts of international terrorism, and (3) the government provides assurances that it will not support international terrorism in the future. Alternatively, the President may lift restrictions if he determines that the government has not supported terrorism in the preceding six months, and has provided assurances that it will not support international terrorism in the future.
Sec. 40A, Arms Export Control Act (22 U.S.C. 2781)	Prohibits the selling or leasing of defense articles or defense services to any country that "is not cooperating fully with United States antiterrorism efforts." Determined annually to apply only to that fiscal year.	President could delist (list comes out annually by May 15). President may waive for a specific transaction if he finds it "important to the national interests of the United States."
Sec. 6, Bretton Woods Agreements Act Amendments, 1978 (22 U.S.C. 286e-11)	Requires the Secretary of the Treasury to instruct U.S. executive directors to the International Monetary Fund "to work in opposition to" loans to any state that permits entry to any person who has committed an act of international terrorism, or otherwise harbors such person.	No waiver. A determination pursuant to sec. 6(j), Export Administration Act of 1979 to remove Cuba from the list of state sponsors of terrorism, however, could indirectly remove this restriction.
Additional Restrictions: Foreign Aid, Trade, and International Financial Institutions Programs		
Sec. 307, Foreign Assistance Act of 1961 (22 U.S.C. 2227)	Withholds a proportion of U.S. contributions to the United Nations and other international programs operating in Cuba (except UNICEF and some International Atomic Energy	No waiver.

Statutory Basis	Restriction	Authority to Lift or Waive
	Agency programs).	
Sec. 498A(b), (c), Foreign Assistance Act of 1961 (22 U.S.C. 2295a)	Prohibits some foreign aid to any government of an independent state of the former Soviet Union that the President determines is providing assistance for, or engaging in nonmarket trade with, the Cuban government.	President may waive if he determines that (1) "it is important to the national interest of the United States" to do so; (2) aid will foster respect for internationally recognized human rights, rule of law, development of democratic governance institutions; (3) aid alleviates results of a disaster; (4) aid is for secondary school programs run by the U.S. Information Agency (USIA).
Sec. 498A(d), Foreign Assistance Act of 1961 (22 U.S.C. 2295a)	Reduces aid to any government of an independent state of the former Soviet Union in proportion with that country's aid to Cuba's intelligence facilities.	President may waive if he determines that it is important to U.S. national security. In the case of Russia, must further determine Russia is not sharing intelligence data with the Cuban government.
Sec. 620(f), Foreign Assistance Act of 1961 (22U.S.C. 2370(f))	Prohibits foreign aid to any Communist country, explicitly naming Cuba.	President may waive if he finds it is vital to the security of the United States, the recipient is not controlled by the "international Communist conspiracy," and aid will promote the independence of the recipient. President may also remove Cuba from the stated list of communist countries for any period of time if he finds it important to U.S. national interests to do so.
Sec. 620(t), Foreign Assistance Act of 1961 (22U.S.C. 2370(t))	Prohibits foreign aid and sales under the Food for Peace Act to any government that has, or with which the United States has, severed diplomatic relations.	Aid and sales may resume when diplomatic relations resume.
Sec. 620(y), Foreign Assistance Act of 1961 (22U.S.C. 2370(y))	Prohibits foreign aid to a third country in amounts equal to that country's providing nuclear fuel and related assistance to Cuba the	Prohibition is lifted when Cuba signs and complies with the Treaty on the Non-proliferation of Nuclear Weapons and the Treaty of Tlatelelco, negotiates full-scope

Table 1. (Continued)

Statutory Basis	Restriction	Authority to Lift or Waive
	previous fiscal year.	safeguards, and is found in compliance with the treaties.
Sec. 2(b)(2), Export-Import Bank Act of 1945 (12 U.S.C. 635(2)(b)(2))	Prohibits Ex-Im Bank funding for Marxist-Leninist states, explicitly naming Cuba.	President may determine Cuba has ceased to be a Marxist-Leninist country. President may determine that a specific transaction, or a transaction of a certain kind, is in the national interest.
Sec. 110, Trafficking Victims Protection Act of 2000 (22 U.S.C. 7107)	Prohibits nonhumanitarian, nontrade-related aid to Cuba for its failure to comply with minimum standards or make significant efforts related to trafficking in persons.	Determination made annually: Secretary of State could find Cuba in compliance the next fiscal year. Secretary of State could make a determination of compliance outside the annual cycle of reporting. The President may continue nonhumanitarian, non-trade-related aid if he finds it would "promote the purposes" of the act or is otherwise in the U.S. national interest.
Sec. 7007, 7015(f), Department of State, Foreign Operations, and Related Programs Appropriations Act, 2015 (Division J, P.L. 113-235)	Sec. 7007: Prohibits direct funding to Cuba. Sec. 7015(f): prohibits aid to Cuba without regular notification procedures of the Committees on Appropriations.	No waivers. The two sections apply only to the current fiscal year.
Sec. 12, International Development Association Act (22 U.S.C. 284j) Sec. 21, Inter-American Development Bank Act (22 U.S.C. 283r)	Requires the President to instruct U.S. executive directors to the relevant international financial institution to oppose loans to any state that has nationalized, expropriated, or seized property owned by a U.S. citizen; canceled contracts with a U.S. citizen; imposed discriminatory taxes that have the result of property seizure.	The President may determine that (1) arrangements for compensation have been made; (2) the issue has been submitted to arbitration; or (3) good faith negotiations are underway.

Statutory Basis	Restriction	Authority to Lift or Waive
Sec. 401, Tariff Classification Act of 1962 (19 U.S.C. 1351 note)	Requires Cuba to be treated as a nation "dominated or controlled by the foreign government or foreign organization controlling the world Communist movement," resulting in denying articles that are "the growth, produce, or manufacture of Cuba" favorable trade terms. The U.S. Harmonized Tariff Schedule (HTS) designates Cuba in the most restricted trade category ("Column 2") pursuant to this provision and other trade laws as follows: "b) Rate of Duty Column 2. Notwithstanding any of the foregoing provisions of this note, the rates of duty shown in column 2 shall apply to products, whether imported directly or indirectly, of the following countries and areas pursuant to section 401 of the Tariff Classification Act of 1962, to section 231 or 257(e)(2) of the Trade Expansion Act of 1962, to section 404(a) of the Trade Act of 1974 or to any other applicable section of law, or to action taken by the President thereunder: Cuba, North Korea."	The restrictions ceases to apply "on or after the date on which the President proclaims that he has determined that Cuba is no longer dominated or controlled" by such a foreign power.
Sec. 401, Trade Act of 1974 (19 U.S.C. 2431)	Continues to deny nondiscriminatory trade treatment for countries that were so denied prior to enactment of this title.	The President may temporarily waive or lift by entering into a bilateral commercial agreement (sec. 405; 19 U.S.C. 2435), and may temporarily extend nondiscriminatory terms (sec. 404; 19 U.S.C. 2434). Granting permanent

Table 1. (Continued)

Statutory Basis	Restriction	Authority to Lift or Waive
		nondiscriminatory trade treatment (Normal Trade Relations, or NTR), however, requires an act of Congress (sec. 151; 19 U.S.C. 2191).
Sec. 402, Trade Act of 1974 (Jackson-Vanik Amendment; 19 U.S.C. 2432)	Continues to deny nondiscriminatory trade treatment for countries that were so denied prior to enactment of this title, including countries under sec. 401, communist countries, or non-market economies (as defined in the Senate report accompanying H.R. 10710, 93rd Congress, enacted as the Trade Act of 1974).	President may suspend temporarily, and may renew the suspension semiannually (by June 30 and December 31) if he determines and notifies Congress that the government of Cuba does not (1) deny its citizens the right or opportunity to emigrate; (2) impose more than a nominal tax on emigration and documents required to emigrate or travel; or (3) impose more than a nominal tax on a citizen as a result of that citizen's desire to emigrate. President may suspend temporarily, with annual renewal, by issuing an executive order stating that (1) waiving will promote the objectives of Jackson-Vanik; and (2) "he has received assurances that the emigration practices of that country will henceforth lead substantially to the achievements of the objectives of the section." Congress may block the President's initial determinations (sec. 152; 19 U.S.C. 2192), or extension of waiver (sec. 153; 19 U.S.C. 2193). Granting permanent nondiscriminatory trade treatment however, requires an act of Congress (sec. 151; 19 U.S.C. 2191). Removal of Jackson-Vanik

Statutory Basis	Restriction	Authority to Lift or Waive
		restrictions, however, does not require NTR status (the President may exercise the above-described waiver authority).
Sec. 502(b), Trade Act of 1974 (19 U.S.C. 2462(b))	A country is denied "beneficiary developing country" status under the Generalized System of Preferences if it is a Communist country, and if it has expropriated property of a U.S. citizen.	President may waive if he finds it in the national economic interest of the United States to do so.
Sec. 212, Caribbean Basin Economic Recovery Act (19 U.S.C. 2702)	Cuba is not eligible for CBERA benefits because it is not listed in sec. 212(b). In addition, a country is denied "beneficiary country" status under the CBERA if it is a Communist country; has nationalized, expropriated, or seized property owned by a U.S. citizen; canceled contracts with a U.S. citizen; imposed discriminatory taxes that have the result of property seizure; fails to recognize certain arbitral awards in favor of a U.S. citizen, corporation, partnership, or corporation; affords preferential treatment to products of a developed country other than the United States (unless there is no significant adverse effect on U.S. commerce); if a government-owned entity engages in the broadcast of U.S.-owned copyrighted material without express consent; is not a signatory to an agreement regarding the extradition of U.S. citizens; and has not or is not taking	Congress would have to amend sec. 212(b) to add Cuba to the list of countries eligible for CBERA designation. Once listed, the President could designate Cuba as beneficiary country, despite other restrictions, if he finds it in the national economic interest of the United States to do so, except if the country affords preferential treatment to products of a developed country other than the United States (unless there is no significant adverse effect on U.S. commerce), and is a signatory to an agreement regarding the extradition of U.S. citizens.

Table 1. (Continued)

Statutory Basis	Restriction	Authority to Lift or Waive
	steps to afford internationally recognized worker rights.	
Sec. 902, Food Security Act of 1985 (7 U.S.C. 1446 note)	Sec. 902, Food Security Act of 1985 (7 U.S.C. 1446 note)	Sec. 204, Cuban Liberty and Democratic Solidarity (LIBERTAD) Act (22 U.S.C. 6064) authorizes the President to suspend the enforcement of sec. 902 if he determines "a transition government is in power in Cuba." Sec. 204, furthermore, requires the President to terminate sanctions under sec. 902 and other measures if he determines that "a democratically elected government in Cuba is in power." Sec. 204(d)(1) of that Act repeals sec. 902 on President making such a determination.
Sec. 211, Omnibus Consolidated and Emergency Supplemental Appropriations Act, 1999 (Division A, Title II, P.L. 105-277)	Prohibits a transaction or payment with respect to a mark, trade, name or commercial name that is the same as or substantially similar to a mark, trade name, or commercial name used in connection with a business or assets that were confiscated. Prohibits U.S. courts from considering or enforcing trademark claims of a Cuba national, or their successor in interest, regarding property confiscated by the Cuban government.	No waiver.

End Notes

[1] 27 Federal Register 1085, February 7, 1962 (Proclamation 3447, Embargo on All Trade with Cuba, February 3, 1962).

[2] Previously, in October 1960 under the Eisenhower Administration, exports to Cuba were placed under strict export controls under the authority of the Export Control Act of 1949 in response to the expropriation of U.S. properties. This in effect amounted to an embargo on exports of all products with the exception of certain foods, medicines, and medical supplies.

[3] 27 Federal Register 1116, February 7, 1962.

[4] 27 Federal Register 2765-2766, March 24, 1962.

[5] 28 Federal Register 6974-6985, July 9, 1963.

[6] 31 C.F.R. §515.533.

[8] Cuba's designation on the state sponsor of terrorism list has allowed U.S. nationals injured by an act of international terrorism to file lawsuits against Cuba in the United States for damages. For more information, see CRS Report WSLG254, Can Victims of Terrorism in the United States Sue Foreign Governments? by Jennifer K. Elsea.

[9] CRS has prepared a memorandum for general distribution on Cuban Assets Control Regulations, with Final Rule of January 16, 2015 Incorporated in Ramseyer Form, available on request from the authors.

[10] 80 Federal Register 2286-2302, January 16, 2015.

[11] U.S. Government Accountability Office, U.S. Embargo On Cuba: Recent Regulatory Changes and Potential Presidential or Congressional Actions, GAO-09-0951R, September 17, 2009.

In: Cuba in Context
Editor: Janet G. Campbell

ISBN: 978-1-63482-985-4

Chapter 3

TESTIMONY OF ROBERTA S. JACOBSON, ASSISTANT SECRETARY OF STATE FOR WESTERN HEMISPHERE AFFAIRS, U.S. DEPARTMENT OF STATE. HEARING ON "UNDERSTANDING THE IMPACT OF U.S. POLICY CHANGES ON HUMAN RIGHTS AND DEMOCRACY IN CUBA"*

Chairman Rubio, Ranking Member Boxer, and Members of the Committee:

Thank you for the opportunity to testify today on our new approach to U.S.- Cuba policy. I know many of you have a deep interest in U.S. policy towards Cuba and have closely followed the President's announcement on December 17 and subsequent events, including my meetings in Havana two weeks ago. I appreciate the Committee's engagement on issues related to Cuba and the Western Hemisphere and applaud your strong commitment to democratic values, human rights, and expanding social and economic opportunity in the Americas.

---

* This is an edited, reformatted and augmented version of testimony presented February 3, 2015 before the Senate Foreign Relations Committee, Subcommittee on Western Hemisphere, Transitional Crime, Civilian Security, Democracy, Human Rights, and Global Women's Issues.

I also want to thank the Committee for its assistance in welcoming the long-overdue return of Alan Gross to his family. During Mr. Gross' five long years of detention, the Administration worked closely with many members of Congress – from both chambers and from both parties – to secure his release. As the President and the Secretary have said, we are also grateful for the essential roles of Canada, Pope Francis, and the Vatican in reaching an agreement that made Mr. Gross' freedom possible.

Our previous approach to relations with Cuba over a half century, though rooted in the best of intentions, failed to empower the Cuban people and isolated us from our democratic partners in this hemisphere and around the world. Additionally, the Cuban government has used this policy as a rationale for restrictions on its people. As a result, unfortunately and unintentionally, those most deprived were the Cuban people.

The President's initiatives look forward and are designed to promote changes that support universal human rights and fundamental freedoms for every Cuban, as well as changes that promote our other national interests. They emphasize the value of people-to-people contact and very specific forms of increased commerce. We are already seeing indications that our updated approach gives us a greater ability to engage other nations in the hemisphere and around the world in promoting respect for fundamental freedoms in Cuba. It has also drawn considerably greater attention to the actions and policies of the Cuban government.

From the beginning of this Administration, our approach has been to implement policies toward Cuba that support the Cuban people in freely determining their own future – their own political and economic future. Because ultimately, it will be the Cuban people themselves who drive political and economic reforms. That is why we lifted restrictions to make it easier for Cuban Americans to travel and send remittances to their families in Cuba, and opened new pathways for academic, religious, and people-to-people exchanges. These changes created powerful new connections between our two countries. The steps we are implementing now build on this foundation by increasing travel, authorized commerce, and the flow of information to, from, and within Cuba. The regulatory changes we announced will increase the financial resources to support the Cuban people and the emerging Cuban private sector. They also enable U.S. companies to expand telecommunications and internet access within Cuba. U.S. policy will no longer be a barrier to connectivity in Cuba.

This Administration is under no illusions about the continued barriers to internationally recognized freedoms that remain for the Cuban people, nor are we under illusions about the nature of the Cuban government. When we sat down with our counterparts in Havana, we were clear that our governments have both shared interests and sharp differences. From mail service to counter narcotics to oil spill mitigation, we owe our people a diplomatic relationship that allows an effective pursuit of their interests. On these types of practical issues, we agreed to continue dialogue and increase cooperation. At the same time, I raised with the Cuban government our concerns about its harassment, use of violence, and arbitrary detention of Cuban citizens peacefully expressing their views. I met with dissidents, entrepreneurs, and independent media voices to talk about what they need from their government and from us.

I talked with my Cuban counterpart about several elements that presently inhibit the work of our U.S. Interests Section, including travel restrictions on our diplomats, limits on staffing and local access to the mission, and problems receiving timely shipments to the mission. The successful resolution of these issues will enable a future U.S. Embassy to provide services commensurate with our other diplomatic missions around the world and on a par with the many foreign diplomatic missions in Cuba. We began a useful discussion and intend to meet again this month.

Having just seen our U.S. diplomats in Havana in action, I would like to take this opportunity to salute their tireless work to advance U.S. interests on the island by conducting educational and cultural diplomacy, monitoring significant political and economic developments, and promoting respect for democracy and human rights, including engaging with Cuba's independent civil society. These dedicated public servants have done their jobs under often very difficult circumstances. Our diplomats unite families through our immigration processing, provide American citizen services, and issue visas for qualified visitors to the United States. Our Refugee Processing Center provides assistance to victims of political repression. Our public diplomacy officers work in partnership with a range of journalists, including those from civil society, and provide hundreds of Cubans each week with uncensored internet access through our three Information Resource Centers. Our consular officers issue tens of thousands of travel documents annually to Cubans traveling to the United States for the purposes of emigrating or visiting friends and family. These efforts will continue and expand once we establish diplomatic relations with Cuba.

We have only begun the official talks on normalizing relations – which will take considerably longer than the first step, which is the re-establishment of diplomatic relations. But even while we do so, we will continue, both directly and through diplomatic channels, to encourage our allies to take every public and private opportunity to support increased respect for human rights and fundamental freedoms in Cuba. We will continue to use funds appropriated by Congress to support the exercise of political and civil liberties in Cuba, facilitate the free flow of information, and provide humanitarian assistance. We also look forward to increased engagement to empower the Cuban people through authorized contact with Members of Congress, U.S. government officials, and American travelers. We encourage Members visiting Cuba to expand their engagement with the independent voices in Cuban civil society and, whenever possible, to engage effectively on human rights and democracy with the Cuban government.

We will continue our discussions with our oversight and appropriations committees as we move toward a new relationship. We appreciate that there is a diversity of views in the U.S. Congress on the new direction towards Cuba. However, we hope that we can also work together to find common ground towards our shared goal of enabling the Cuban people to freely determine their own future.

We appreciate your attention to these important issues. Thank you and I welcome your questions.

In: Cuba in Context
Editor: Janet G. Campbell

ISBN: 978-1-63482-985-4

Chapter 4

TESTIMONY OF TOM P. MALINOWSKI, ASSISTANT SECRETARY OF STATE FOR DEMOCRACY, HUMAN RIGHTS, AND LABOR, U.S. DEPARTMENT OF STATE. HEARING ON "UNDERSTANDING THE IMPACT OF U.S. POLICY CHANGES ON HUMAN RIGHTS AND DEMOCRACY IN CUBA"*

Mr. Chairman, Ranking Member, and Members of the Committee: Thank you for the opportunity to testify today, and to share my thoughts about how we can best stand up for the human rights and fundamental freedoms of the Cuban people.

It is plain from the debate that followed the President's announcement of our new policy that people who feel passionately about freedom for the Cuban people can disagree passionately about how best to advance it. I have long been committed to this cause, and I believe with all my heart that the President chose the right course. I have listened with great care and respect to those who disagree, and while I will try to address their concerns today, I want to be clear that I do not dismiss them.

I want to start by making a few points on which I hope we all agree.

---

* This is an edited, reformatted and augmented version of testimony presented February 3, 2015 before the Senate Foreign Relations Committee, Subcommittee on Western Hemisphere, Transitional Crime, Civilian Security, Democracy, Human Rights, and Global Women's Issues.

First, the promotion of universal human rights and the empowerment of all Cubans must be the bedrock of our policy toward Cuba. President Obama has made clear that it will be. And here, we will take our cues from the Cuban people, supporting their vision for Cuba's future. As Secretary Kerry has said, we support the key points around which Cuban civil society groups have rallied:

- Cuban ratification and compliance with various UN human rights treaties;
- Recognition of independent civil society;
- Implementation of constitutional and legal reforms to ensure full respect for labor rights, freedoms of expression, association, peaceful assembly, and
- expression, and to allow for free elections;
- Release of prisoners arrested for political reasons; and
- An end to government-sponsored harassment of independent civil society.

Second, the most immediate result of this policy shift – the release from prison of 53 activists who are now back with their families and able to continue their brave work – is unambiguously a good thing. The released men and women included all Cubans designated by Amnesty International as "prisoners of conscience," and many known to my Bureau to have been prosecuted for peaceful expression, association, and assembly in Cuba. Among them is independent rapper "El Critico," arrested after a government-organized counter protest retaliated against him for painting anti-government messages on his home and distributing pro-democracy pamphlets; Ivan Fernandez Depestre, arrested for the absurd offense of "precriminal dangerousness," a label the government uses to detain people in anticipation of crimes that supposedly are yet to be committed; and Sonia Garro, who can march again on Sundays with her fellow Ladies in White. We will spare no effort to ensure that everyone still detained for simply exercising their rights to freedom of expression, association, or peaceful assembly is free, not just from prison but from harassment, threats and restrictions on their movement and their work.

Third, we agree that the release of these political prisoners does not of itself change anything in Cuba. Cuba remains a one-party state that tries to stifle virtually all political, cultural and economic activity that it does not control. The government continues to crack down on everything from art performances in Havana squares, to independent meetings by civil society out in the provinces. It continues to employ short-term detentions – at times with violence – to disrupt free expression and peaceful assembly, and has used this tactic since President Obama's announcement, including against recently released political prisoners. No one should have any illusions about the nature of this system, or about the determination of the current leadership to keep things just as they are for as long as possible.

And let's be clear: none of this, Cuba's repression, its poverty, its isolation, is the fault of the United States or of the embargo. The responsibility lies with the Cuban government, period.

At the same time, after 50 years of experience with the embargo, we have to face the hard truth that it has not weakened the repressive apparatus of the Castro government. It has not strengthened Cuba's civil society. It has not given us the leverage we need to press for change, or the Cuban people the hope they crave. The Castro government has been happy in its isolation. The Cuban people have not.

I say this as someone who often supports economic sanctions to leverage progress for human rights. I completely agree with Senator Rubio that no country ever became a democracy simply because of trade and tourists.

At the same time, over many years of working on this issue, I have seen how the Castro government has turned our policy against us, and how this has helped an authoritarian form of government survive so close to our shores long after walls of repression from Berlin to Moscow to our own hemisphere came tumbling down.

For decades, in capitals around the world, the Cuban government has succeeded in making our embargo and its isolation from the United States a bigger issue than its own repression, making it difficult to mobilize international pressure to improve respect for human rights on the island. To its own people, the government has justified Cuba's isolation, poverty and lack of democracy as being a result of American hostility. These were bad excuses; they justified none of what the Cuban people have suffered all these years. But we have to acknowledge that, over the years, shifting the blame to America has worked for the Castro government.

It is not going to work any more.

Now, every country in Latin America and the Caribbean, and indeed around the world, knows that the United States is not the obstacle to Cuba's integration with the hemisphere and its prospects for economic development. Cuban policies are the obstacle. Now every citizen of Cuba knows that the U.S. is willing to have improved relations with their country, to support private business on the island and to help connect them to the world. These steps have raised the Cuban people's expectations, and shifted the burden of meeting those expectations back upon the Cuban state.

The Cuban government can respond in one of two ways. It can begin the reforms needed for its people to benefit from the opening to the U.S. – by allowing greater Internet access, for example, and easing restrictions on private businesses, on travel, and on civil society – in which case the Cuban people will be less dependent on their government and will have more power to shape their future. This is what we hope will happen. Or it can keep resisting those reforms, in which case it will further lose domestic and international legitimacy, because Cubans and others in the international community will know exactly who is to blame for their country's problems.

Critics of our new policy have argued that we gave away leverage by easing restrictions on engagement with Cuba without demanding democratic reforms up front. But the Cuban government did not ask for and is not necessarily eager for us to take the steps the president announced, which involve efforts to get more information and resources to Cuban civil society and private citizens, and greater access to Cuba and its people for our diplomats. It should go without saying that the Cuban government wasn't going to stop repressing its people in exchange for Americans connecting its people to the internet. These steps were not tradable commodities, but actions we took in our own interest, to help ordinary Cubans, and to shift the attention of the world to the embargo that matters – the one the Cuban government has imposed on its own people.

Our new policy has opened these new opportunities to engage with the Cuban people; we will now work energetically to seize them and to advance them. In doing so, we will continue to consult with independent Cuban civil society to hear their views and plans for the future activities. And we will urge other countries to join us in pressing the Cuban government on human rights and democracy.

We have reengaged nations throughout our hemisphere on the importance of supporting genuine progress on human rights and democratic principles in Cuba as a means to advance meaningful and principled regional integration. Last week, I attended the inauguration of Bolivian President Morales where I had the opportunity to meet with leaders and foreign ministers from throughout the Hemisphere to stress the importance of ensuring we speak with a united voice on Cuba. The common reaction was that we had taken a giant step for the Hemisphere and that the time had come to encourage Cuba to do its part.

We are also working with our friends in the region, and directly with the Government of Panama, to ensure that independent civil society, including independent voices from Cuba, can engage meaningfully with governments at the coming Summit of the Americas. I hope to be at the Summit and meet with Cuban civil society, as well as other civil society representatives, particularly those who find themselves threatened by repressive governments.

We are also deepening our engagement with Europe to encourage partners there to push for advances in human rights and democratic principles with their Cuban counterparts. We have engaged with European delegations here, and I plan to travel to Europe personally to further these discussions. As you know, efforts by the Vatican were critical to the successful negotiation that secured the release of Alan Gross and of the 53 imprisoned Cuban activists, and we will continue to work with the Vatican to encourage the Cuban government to follow through on its other commitments. We will also encourage the EU to press for concrete improvements in human rights in their discussions with Havana and to support the agenda of independent civil society on the island. No government – neither that of the Castros nor those of third countries – can credibly make the case that pushing the Cuban government to respect universal human rights is taking sides in a dispute between Cuba and the United States.

We are also looking for new and innovative ways to responsibly support the emergence of a Cuban private sector as a critical component of civil society. We also envision a role for Latin American and European countries to create links between private small businesses in Cuba and the small businesses in their regions.

Cubans are also entitled to access uncensored information, including through the internet. As Assistant Secretary Jacobson noted, the Administration's regulatory changes will help U.S. and international telecommunications companies provide internet service to the island. These regulatory changes respond directly to requests made to the Administration by civil society to facilitate greater access to telecommunications equipment on the island. The Castro government can no longer argue that its failure to provide internet access to all Cuban citizens is somehow the responsibility of the United States. And we hope Latin American and European companies can cooperate in our efforts to promote the free flow of information to, from, and within the island.

We are also asking other countries to encourage the Cuban government to allow greater access by the United Nations and other international organizations. These actors will provide much needed transparency and are widely seen as credible, objective observers. Cuban dissidents have emphasized the important role that the United Nations can play in advancing human rights in Cuba, and we will use the new opportunities presented by our Cuba policy to mobilize others in the UN and other multilateral fora in support.

The Cuban government has proposed bilateral talks on human rights, and I look forward to leading the U.S. team to these talks. Our objective in such talks will be to develop an agenda of specific reforms that will bring about concrete improvements in compliance with applicable international human rights obligations and commitments. The Cuban side will of course raise its usual allegations about problems in the United States, and I will be proud to defend our record. But we are not interested in an abstract debate; we will continue such talks only if they chart a course for concrete progress on human rights and democratic principles in Cuba. And we will insist that the most important dialogue the Cuban government should have on human rights is with its own people.

President Obama has also made it clear that the U.S. government will continue programs that promote the realization of human rights and fundamental freedoms such as freedoms of peaceful expression, association, and assembly in Cuba, just as we do in 95 countries around the world. These programs are a fundamental part of our human rights policy and national security interests around the world. The Cuban government may continue to object to these efforts, and to try to crack down on those involved with their implementation. But it will find it harder to treat contacts with the U.S. government and with international NGOs as criminal when Cubans see their own leaders engaging in diplomatic relations with us. In any case, we will continue to manage our programs in Cuba with appropriate discretion to protect human rights activists from further reprisal, even as we ask the Cuban government to stop punishing its citizens for activities considered a normal part of life in most other countries. We greatly value the input and coordination of this Committee on our programs and we look forward to further conversations.

Of course, none of this will be easy. If I am right, and our new policy succeeds in empowering the Cuban people to shape their political destiny, then the Cuban government may respond by cracking down harder in the short run but the Cuban people will have the best opportunity in more than half a century to freely determine their own future in the long run.

None of us can say what will happen next. Some of Cuba's bravest dissidents – voices we profoundly respect – believe that we've made a mistake and that nothing good is likely to come from these changes. I hope critics of our policy will acknowledge that others in Cuba who have sacrificed for the cause of democracy believe just as strongly that we have done the right thing. There are many different views on this question, because the future is uncertain.

I'll close by suggesting that this sudden uncertainty, after decades of absolute, depressing certainty that nothing can change, constitutes progress. It carries with it a sense of possibility; an opportunity for debate. This is what most of the Cubans we've heard from in recent days are saying; they don't know if the changes we've announced will bring better days or not, but they feel that something better is at least possible now.

Reinaldo Escobar, a journalist who began his career writing for official Cuban government media and now writes for the independent Cuban news outlet 14ymedio, summed up this feeling in an essay he titled "A New Dawn:"

The entire world, he wrote, now "has its eyes set on the government of Cuba ... They know it and will have to choose between loosening the repression or letting the world down. I am betting that they will let the world down, but I am hoping to lose the bet. All the signs and accumulated experience clearly say that this is only a new maneuver to win some time and to allow them to get away with their schemes, but this is also an unprecedented move and things can always turn out differently. The most important thing is that the domino game has been shaken up and it is time to move the pieces."

Mr. Chairman, members of the Committee, having shaken up the game, we have a chance now to help things turn out differently for the Cuban people. I hope we can work together to seize that chance.

INDEX

D

E

F

N

O

P

R

W